SAFE IN THE ARMS OF Jesus

The Story of Fanny Crosby

SAFE IN THE ARMS of Jesus

Chester & S. Ann Hearn

CHRISTIAN · LITERATURE · CRUSADE
Fort Washington, Pennsylvania 19034

CHRISTIAN LITERATURE CRUSADE

U.S.A.
P.O. Box 1449, Fort Washington, PA 19034

GREAT BRITAIN
51 The Dean, Alresford, Hants., SO24 9BJ

AUSTRALIA
P.O. Box 419M, Manunda, QLD 4879

NEW ZEALAND
10 MacArthur Street, Feilding

ISBN 0-87508-665-9

Copyright © 1998
Chester G. Hearn and S. Ann Hearn

This printing 1998

PRINTED IN THE UNITED STATES OF AMERICA

Table of Contents

Chapter   Page

1. "Oh, What a Happy Child I Am" 7

2. Escape from Ignorance 21

3. Teacher and Poet 35

4. Reaching Out 47

5. Now She Belonged to Him 61

6. "There's Music in the Air" 71

7. The Bradbury Years 83

8. Hymns for the Ages 99

9. Leading Souls to Christ 111

10. Thirty More Years 125

    Afterword 141

In memory of
our beloved daughter,
Wendy

— 1 —

"Oh, What a Happy Child I Am"

*O*n March 24, 1820, as the first winds of spring swept across the southeast corner of Putnam County, New York, Mercy Crosby gave birth to her first child—Frances Jane. They called her Fanny, and her little hands, like those of all newborns, clutched at the air as she lay beside her happy mother. John, her father, looked lovingly into the child's sparkling blue eyes and proudly declared, "She is a Crosby." Though thinking of himself, his statement took nothing away from the mother, whose maiden name was also Crosby, but of a different family.

The days passed with great joy in the home, and as the fields dried, John began the spring planting. In the evenings he sat beside the hearth and gently held the child. She followed his fingers as they danced before her eyes, laughing and grasping as the two of them played. "Our Fanny is a bright little child," said John to his wife. "What a wonderful blessing from the Lord."

"Yes," she replied, "and one so very precious."

But one morning in late April, Mercy Crosby went to the cradle and noticed pus forming in her daughter's eyes. "Fanny has a cold," she declared, and when the condition became worse, she urged her husband to get the doctor.

John departed on his fastest horse, only to return hours later. "The doctor is away," he said glumly, "and will not be back for several days."

As Mercy gently dabbed a warm, moist cloth over Fanny's pasted eyelids, she glared at her husband and said sternly, "Well, try to find another! Our daughter is sick!"

John remounted and hours later returned with a young physician who had just opened an office in a nearby town. The doctor had never treated an eye inflammation, but he knew of poultices that cured other types of infections and prescribed a hot compress. When the mixture touched Fanny's eyes, she cried with pain, thrashing her little arms and kicking her feet, but the doctor nodded approvingly.

"It is a natural reaction," he said. "She will be well in a day or two."

But all was not well. The infection soon cleared, but Fanny's eyes no longer followed the fingers of her playful father or hungrily watched as her mother came to nurse her. The bright sunny world had suddenly turned black. Fanny

Crosby, six weeks old, would never see again.
The doctor, horrified at what he had done, left
the county, and John Crosby—stricken with
grief—lamented, "What kind of life can a blind
girl have?" Then, with tears running down his
cheeks, he turned to his wife and asked, "Who
will want our precious Fanny?"

John died before his daughter reached the
age of one. Had he lived a full life, he would
have learned the answers to his questions. Precious little Fanny fell into good hands. God
wanted her for a special kind of work.

As she began to grow, her sense of hearing, tasting, smelling, and feeling each became
sharpened and honed. Her mother read to her
every day, always from the Bible. She knew the
eyes of her daughter would forever shut out all
the beauties of nature, and she prayed that the
darkness would be overcome by a deep abiding
faith in the Lord.

One day, while they were sitting together,
Mercy said to Fanny, "Two of the world's greatest poets are blind. At times the Lord takes from
a person something physical in order to awaken
a greater spiritual insight." And then she read
from Milton's sonnet on his blindness:

When I consider how my light is spent
Ere half my days in this dark world and
    wide,
And that one talent which is death to
    hide
Lodged with me useless, though my soul
    more bent
To serve therewith my Maker, and present
My true account, lest He returning chide,
"Doth God exact day labor, light denied?"
I fondly ask. But Patience, to prevent
That murmur, soon replies: "God doth not
    need
Either man's work or his own gifts; who
    best
Bear His mild yoke, they serve Him best;
    His state
Is kingly; thousands at His bidding speed
And post o'er land and ocean without rest;
They also serve who only stand and wait."

Poetry touched Fanny's senses like the
sweet fragrance of summer roses, the tang of sharp
cheeses, and the twitter of scolding wrens. She
drew strength from the great rock by the brook
that she sat on, listening to the harmonizing of
God's great creation. In those quiet moments
the Psalms of David flowed through her thoughts.

The music of the Lord seemed to swell inside her: she could feel the colors and fragrances all about her—the green pastures, spring violets, red-breasted robins, a drove of sheep dotting a distant meadow.

"I soon learned what other children possessed," Fanny recalled, "but I made up my mind to store away a little jewel in my heart, which I called Contentment. This became the comfort of my whole life."

Even as a three-year-old, her sense of the physical world began to overcome her blindness. Grandmother Crosby came often, and, sitting with Fanny on the rocking chair, she spoke of the miracle of God's great sun—its power to grow and nourish all things, to touch the sky with crimson at sunset, and to give way to night's soft carpet of twinkling stars. "Of the shining moon," Fanny recalled, "Grandma gave me such descriptions as I never forgot, and the clouds of day with their shapes and colors were made real to me by her."

Fanny learned from her grandmother the greatness of nature, its power and its gentleness. Once, after a thunderstorm, she took her grandmother's hand and followed her to the brow of a hill. "Oh, Fanny," she said, "there is such a beautiful bow in the heavens. It has seven colors. I wish you could see it: it is a sign of God's covenant of mercy to this world."

Fanny turned her face to the rainbow and concentrated on imagining its colors, as descriptive words spilled gently and brightly from the lips of her grandmother. "The colors," Fanny declared, "are all very real to me."

During the early years, Grandma Crosby taught of birds and their habits—the rat-a-tat-tat of the red-headed woodpecker, the haunting coo of the dove, and the rasping caw of the crow in the corn patch. With spring came the fragrance of apple blossoms, tulips, and daffodils. And with summer the roses, the hollyhocks, and the hum of bees. Fanny touched the flowers, felt their fragile blossoms, held them to her nose, and sniffed the delicious aroma. Her sense of smell became so keen that she could walk into an unfamiliar and cluttered garden and name the herbs and flowers.

One day Fanny told her mother, "I see things because they are there, but I do not know them as one with sight."

Mercy Crosby understood and one evening brought home a tiny motherless lamb. Fanny grasped it and gently ran her fingers through the warm, wooly coat.

"A lamb!" she cried with joy. "I'll be its

mother and call it Fanny's little lamb."

"There's something I'd like to read to you," her mother said, and for the first time in Fanny's life, she listened to "Mary's Little Lamb."

As the story fell upon her ears, Fanny imagined herself and her lamb going to school and playing in the fields. For many months they rambled down by the brook or fell asleep together under the great oak tree. They became great friends, but the lamb grew much faster and stronger than Fanny. It gnawed on Fanny's clothes, and Mrs. Crosby feared that it might injure her daughter. One day it disappeared, and when Fanny learned that her mother had sold her pet to the butcher, she cried for days. At bedtime she knelt and fervently prayed, "Heavenly Father, please bless my little lamb."

The lamb never returned, and the loss became another turning point in Fanny's childhood. Life, filled with so many splendors, also contained great tragedies, and for sympathy and understanding she always turned to her grandmother.

"Mother read from the Bible every day," Fanny recalled, "but it was Grandma who brought the Bible to me, and me to the Bible. The stories of the Holy Book came from her lips and entered my heart and took great root there."

Those moments, more than any other, became the foundation that molded Fanny Crosby's life. "When evening shadows fell, Grandma would take me alone and, rocking me in her old chair, tell me of a kind heavenly Father who sent His only son Jesus Christ down into this world to be a Saviour and a Friend to all mankind. Then she taught me to kneel in prayer, and often I bowed my weary little head and sightless eyes in Grandma's lap and fell asleep."

The memory of the hours spent with Grandma on her rocking chair stayed with Fanny all her life. Years later, she put those recollections fondly into verse:

> I am thinking of a cottage,
> On a quiet rural dell,
> And a brook that ran beside it,
> That I used to love so well.
> I have sat for hours and listened,
> While it rippled at my feet,
> And I thought no other music
> In the world was half so sweet.

Fanny drew strength from her grandmother. Others told her, "Oh, you cannot do this—because you are blind," or, "You can never go there, because it would not be worthwhile—you could not see anything if you did." But her grandmother taught her courage and faith, and encouraged boundless ambition to overcome her handicap.

"As a girl," Fanny recalled, "I lived many lives with my imagination. Sometimes I was a sailor, standing at the masthead and looking into the storm; sometimes a general, leading armies to battle; then a clergyman, addressing large audiences and pleading with them to come to Christ; then the leader of a gigantic choir of voices, singing praises to God."

In her mind, Fanny decided that she would devote her life to some great purpose. But she asked herself, "How can a poor blind girl, with ambition but without influential friends, possibly achieve anything? The great world is rushing past me day by day and sweeping on toward goals I can't imagine, while I will be left stranded by the wayside."

Thoughts of the future often left her depressed, and she would creep out of the cottage to the great rock she called Comfort. There she would kneel and pray, asking God if she was one of His children, even though she was blind. "In all Your world," she prayed, "is there not some little place for me?" It often seemed that she could hear Him say, "Do not be discouraged, little girl. You shall someday be happy and useful, even in your blindness."

Praying revived her spirit, and Fanny gradually began to lose her regret for having been robbed of sight. Little by little, God's promises and consolations took hold in her life. Scriptures, and the hymns sung on the Sabbath, burned themselves into her memory. Her finely tuned hearing could pick out the words of hymns, no matter how indistinctly sung. She knew that Scripture verses came from the Bible, but she began to wonder who created those marvelous hymns. They lifted her up, filling her soul with joy. In her young mind she wondered whether she herself could ever write one that people would sing.

One day in 1825, while romping outdoors, she heard her mother call and rushed to the cottage. "Fanny," she said, "I am going to take you on a little journey." Like Grandma Crosby, Fanny's mother always tried to paint every event like a picture. "We shall travel first in a wagon, till we come to the bank of a beautiful river, with mountains on each side of it. Then we shall get onto a boat and sail for many miles and come to a great city—larger than anything you could imagine—and stay there for several days. And then home again."

The anticipation of taking a journey filled Fanny with joy. "I danced about the room with perhaps not enough attention to the furniture that kept getting in the way until Mother explained the object of the trip—to have a surgical operation performed on my eyes."

"There may be some pain with it, Fanny," warned her mother, "but you are willing to bear it, are you not?"

Fanny hesitated. She already knew enough about pain to last her a lifetime, and she had grown accustomed to blindness.

"But Fanny," her mother argued, "perhaps it will result in giving you sight so that you can see everything around you and play with children, read interesting books, and enjoy yourself in a hundred ways not possible now."

Fanny nodded, thinking the trip might be an answer to her prayers, and the prospect of sight made her happy again.

The journey down the Hudson River filled her with new sensations. She felt the presence of many bodies, the passing richness of scenery, and the smell of the river. Though her mother became seasick, Fanny remained the "gayest of the gay" and quickly mastered the deck. She so amazed the captain with her nimbleness that he made her "first mate of the sloop." She did not even know how she looked, though others called her "a fairly pretty child with black curls and frisky manners" and named her "the belle of the boat."

Disembarking at New York, Fanny discovered a city humming with new sounds, all melded together in a rush and a roar. Soon they were in the presence of the famous Dr. Valentine Mott, who occupied the chair of surgery at Columbia College.

"Mother stood in awe of Dr. Mott," Fanny recalled, "and with bated breath she listened to his every word. I sensed that he had a kind, pleasant face, but I remained doubtful he could do much for me. A little later he examined my eyes with Dr. Delafield and told Mother there was no hope—malpractice had spoiled them."

After the verdict, Fanny heard her mother weeping. She truly did not want to be the cause of her mother's sorrow. But when the doctor placed a fatherly hand on her head and patted it, saying, "Poor little girl!"—Fanny resented it. Blindness was not new to her. She could live with it.

Homeward bound, Fanny curled up in her bunk on the sloop and listened to the waves slapping against the hull. She found a pleasant rhythm in the sound, as if the river were singing only to her: "Fanny, be brave! Fanny, be brave! Brighter days will come!" It was God's voice she thought she heard—not the river waves, but His voice.

Feeling no sorrow she returned home filled with fresh inspiration. She knew the Lord was with her and would guide her way. He was in her heart; He would be her eyes. She submitted to Him, and three years later, feeling urged to write, she composed her first poem:

> Oh, what a happy child I am,
>   Although I cannot see!
> I am resolved that in this world
>   Contented I will be.
>
> How many blessings I enjoy
>   That other people don't!
> So weep or sigh because I'm blind,
>   I cannot, nor I won't!

Fanny Crosby was eight years old, and she never looked back—only forward.

— 2 —

Escape from Ignorance

*W*hen Fanny turned nine, Mrs. Crosby moved to Ridgefield, Connecticut, where a number of families by the name of Hawley lived. Mrs. Hawley, whom Fanny described as "an old Puritan Presbyterian," took an interest in the child's education and—using "thees" and "thous" —set out to teach her the Bible.

"Mrs. Hawley loved at the same time the green meadows and singing brooks of my imagination," Fanny recalled, "and because of her help, by the time I reached the age of ten, I could recite the first five books of the Old Testament, many psalms, and most of the New Testament."

Fanny also memorized many secular poems and learned the music of rhyme. For a ten-year-old, combining them challenged her mind and was fun. She discovered that what she could not see, she could paint in words—the fragrance of a rose, the singing of wind in the trees, the chirp of sparrows, and the love of God. As verses formed in her mind, she recited them from memory. She could not write, and the chore of committing little poems line by line to paper fell to her mother. Mrs. Hawley acted as literary critic and decided they were "very good," so off the verses went to Grandfather Crosby for a more learned opinion.

Fanny waited to hear from the revered grandfather, and finally the long-sought commentary came. Mercy Crosby opened the letter and—from her father's scrawled handwriting—read silently, "We indeed have a poet in the family, and if Fanny improves as she ought to do, she will be an honor to the whole family. But," he added cautiously, "you must not tell her this, or it will make her proud and spoil her." Mercy honored her father's request and said nothing to Fanny, but a few weeks later the old gentleman visited his granddaughter and told her himself.

Knowledge that she, a blind girl, could compose poetry only strengthened her resolve to find a way to overcome her handicap. "There was one terrible hunger that afflicted me all the years of my youth," she later admitted, "and that was for knowledge—knowledge—knowledge. I felt that there were a million things that I ought to know, and no means of learning them."

Though Fanny accepted her burden of

blindness, she resented being unable to read or write. In the early 1800s, few books existed with raised letters, and those that did were much too expensive. So night after night Fanny went to bed weeping. "I could not drink from the waters of knowledge," she lamented, "that I knew were surging all around me." So she prayed, day by day, "Dear God, please give me light!"—not the power to see, but mental light. And she prayed for an education, always asking herself, "But how am I to get it?"

Fanny knew that country schools could do little for her, but she never doubted that God would find a way. "I always rose from my knees," she recalled, "feeling that these prayers would be answered."

Five years passed, and Fanny never faltered in her prayers to God. During those years she enriched her life with verse, drawing ever closer to the Lord. To Him she felt spiritually bonded, and though her prayers seemed unanswered, she said, "How much better it is to pray, hopefully and with faith, for those things we need, than to fret and complain because we do not already possess them."

But God had been listening, and in His great love and generosity gave guidance to Fanny's mother.

"What a thrill ran through me," Fanny declared, "when Mother announced that arrangements had been made for me to attend the school for the blind in New York City. Mother spoke only a few words, but what a flood of happiness they emitted to the poor, sad little soul that had so long pined and prayed for knowledge. God had responded to my prayer through His own means, and by His own faithful helpers."

The great news came, however, as a mixed blessing. She must now leave her mother and the many dear friends she had come to love. With eyes that could not see, she must go into a world of people she did not know. With both sadness and joy, Fanny departed on March 3, 1835, for New York. When she arrived at the wharf four days later, she felt the first pangs of homesickness. Dr. John Denison Russ, Superintendent of the New York Institute for the Blind, cordially greeted her and tried to make her feel comfortable.

A Yale graduate, thirty-four-year-old Dr. Russ understood suffering. In 1826 he had witnessed it in Greece, where he remained three years to establish a hospital. Returning to New York in 1834, he began at his own expense the instruction of six blind boys. A year later he came to the institution, learned of Fanny, and knew he must have her. She soon discovered that Dr. Russ and the great poet Lord Byron had been close friends in Greece. To Fanny, a relationship such as this meant that Dr. Russ must also be a poet. If so, he could teach her to become a better one. Convinced that her long wait had not been in vain, she accepted her good fortune as a blessing from God. From the beginning of her prayers more than five years ago, the Lord had made a special place for her in this very special school.

But the first night at the Institute filled her with loneliness. In this unfamiliar new "home," nothing in her room seemed to be in place. She sat on her trunk, forcing back tears and trying to be brave. The door opened, and she heard an adult enter the room. A pair of loving arms wrapped themselves around her thin body, and the soothing voice of a Quaker mother spoke softly and gently.

"Fanny," said the comforting matron, "I guess thee hath never been away from home before."

"No, ma'am," replied Fanny. "Please excuse me. I must cry."

And so she did, letting out the tears until her sobs filled the hallway—drawing another girl into the room to give her comfort.

In the morning she began a journey that lasted forty years. She called the Institute her "happy home," but at the very beginning she quickly discovered that school entailed more than composing verses. Looming up "like a great monster" was arithmetic. Nor did she always find the food as tasty as her mother's home cooking. So in a short parody, she wrote:

> I loathe, abhor, detest, despise
> Those pastry-wrecks, dried apple pies,
> I loathe, abhor, it makes me sick
> To hear the word Arithmetic!

Fanny could do nothing to improve the food, but she resolved to conquer arithmetic—"this great foe to my peace of mind"—and went at it with a vengeance. She soon realized that through all the affairs of life not much could be accomplished without consulting addition, subtraction, multiplication, and division. "Our toil in Arithmetic," she recalled, "was aided by metal slates with holes in them, which we used to count until sums could be formed in our heads." She made the work a swinging, rhymeless sort of poetry in the form of blank verse. She never completely mastered the course, admitting that:

Multiplication is vexation,
  Division is bad;
The rule of three puzzles me,
  And fractions make me mad.

Anna Smith, who became one of Fanny's closest companions, attempted to tutor her in multiplication and division. Finding that Fanny had little aptitude for numbers, Anna informed Dr. Russ, and he unwisely excused Fanny from the subject. "From that hour I was a new creature," Fanny recalled. "What a nightmare I was escaping."

Then came grammar, philosophy, music, science, and history—all given in the form of lectures and readings. Fanny grasped every word, digesting even the most complicated subjects and tucking the knowledge away in her memory. Most amazing of all, she absorbed astronomy with a passion. Having never seen the twinkle of a star, the bloom of a harvest moon, or the march of the constellation Orion across the winter sky, Fanny nevertheless felt filled with their light— just from the way her grandmother had spoken of them in such detail.

She also struggled with perhaps the most important course taught at the Institute—Braille, without which she could not read. She finally got through passages from the Bible, *The Pilgrim's Progress*, and "The Rime of the Ancient Mariner," but only with great patience and much labor. Fanny could recognize a person by the slightest touch of the hand, but Braille baffled her. When quite young, she had taught herself to play the guitar—and now she blamed the strings for putting calluses on her fingertips that hardened her touch.

As the months passed, Fanny stole time every day to compose poetry, but she also began to think of her future. She wanted to become self-reliant and able to help her mother, who struggled with finances to keep her in school. "I have made up my mind to be a teacher," she told Dr. Russ, "and to do so as soon as I can." He gave her encouragement, but then he suddenly left the Institute, creating a great void in her life.

In 1836 Dr. Silas Jones became the school's new superintendent. One morning he entered the classroom and announced, "I would like to have Fanny Crosby come with me for a few minutes."

With a reputation already established as the Institute's young poet, Fanny expected Dr. Jones to ask her to write a poem to honor the visit of some special person or to commemorate a special occasion. Instead, Jones gently said, "Fanny, your attempts at poetry have brought you into prominence here in the school, and a great deal of flattery has been the result. Shun a flatterer, Fanny, as you would a snake! Now I am going to give you some clean truth, which may hurt just now, but will be of great use one of these days."

Fanny steeled herself for a shock she had not expected.

"As yet," the superintendent said, "you know very little about poetry, or, in fact, anything else—compared to what there is to be known. You have almost all of it yet to learn. Do not think too much about rhymes and the praises that come from them. Store your mind with useful knowledge and think more of what you can be than of how you can appear. The favor and laudation of the world, Fanny, is a very fragile thing upon which to depend. Try to merit the approval of God, and of yourself, as well as that of your fellow-creatures."

The words were gentle, but they sounded harsh. As they spilled from Dr. Jones's lips, Fanny tried to understand them. Dr. Russ had never talked to her this way.

"Remember," the new superintendent said kindly, "that the very air you breathe—the very food you eat—the ability or talent that you may develop—all come from God. You are always in His presence and have no right to be vain for a single moment when standing before the great Creator of all things."

"At the end of five minutes," Fanny later recalled, "he had convinced me that instead of becoming a great poet, I was really an ignorant young schoolgirl, who as yet knew scarcely anything whatever. His words were bombshells in the camp of my self-congratulatory thoughts, but they did me an immense amount of good."

As she did with every important event in her life, Fanny quickly processed the advice. Something inside her said, "He tells the truth, Fanny, and it is all for your benefit."

When the hot tears stopped rolling down her cheeks, she touched her way around his chair, put her arms around his neck, and kissed him on the forehead. "You have talked to me as my father, were he living," she said, "and I thank you for it, over and over again. You have given me a lesson that I might have had to learn through bitter experience, and I shall profit by it."

Among the many things Fanny learned at school were the names of hundreds of individuals who achieved fame though blind. Homer, the greatest poet of antiquity, lost his sight while writing the *Odyssey*. Virgil, William Tell, and the great English poet John Milton also became afflicted, but not before they had seen the world. Others, like Francis Huber in the field of science, also became role models for the students at the New York Institute for the Blind. Dr. Jones brought new resolve and purpose to all his students, teaching them that anything within the average power of man or woman they could, with God's help, do—the same as if they had the blessing of sight. "And," said Fanny, "at it we went with a will."

Toiling day and night, she often wondered whether people with sight could understand how a blind person could work intellectually. "Better perhaps than one who can see," she decided. She found it unnecessary to write anything down and helped others to develop the skill. "Memory, when cultivated," she said, "grows a wonderful treasure house of ripened grain." And gradually, at the age of eighteen, Fanny Crosby began to tutor others.

Blindness did not curb some students from practicing pranks. They played little tricks on each other and hazed incoming students. Fanny's fun came from performing in plays and musicals. She remembered her own first sad day at school and refrained from hazing new students. Instead, she tried to give comfort to those in need of loving arms.

This did not prevent her and a younger friend from stealing into the school garden to snatch a watermelon. They had heard that all the melons were to be sold to benefit the school, but having worked in the garden all summer, Fanny did not think it fair to be entirely deprived of the fruit of their hard labor. Some of the boys had already stolen from the melon patch, so Mr. Stevens, the gardener, had volunteered to act as a night watchman. While Fanny occupied the attention of Mr. Stevens, her accomplice carried off a big melon and took it to Fanny's room. News of the robbery brought all the girls to Fanny's quarters, where, but for the rind and seeds, they happily consumed the fruit. It seemed great fun at the time, but later Fanny felt obliged to confess the theft. When the superintendent heard the story, he gave a hearty laugh and said, "To think that you blind children were all getting the better of us 'seeing' people!"

At home, in February 1838, other events were taking place. Mercy Crosby, who had moved to Bridgeport, met and married Thomas Morris, a widower with two daughters and a son. Fanny suddenly found her life merged with little siblings she had never met. In 1840 her mother gave birth to Wilhelmina. The child died in infancy, and Fanny—knowing how her own blindness had given so much pain to her mother—considered it a great tragedy. But the following year brought Julia into the world, a healthy little girl everyone called Julie, and Fanny thanked God for this special blessing. On Christmas Day, 1843, Carolyn was born. Fanny now had family, and during all the years of her long life, her two dearest friends would be Carrie and Julie, her half-sisters.

Fanny enjoyed short vacations with her new family and quickly learned to love them all. She kept them in her prayers and always became sad when starting back to school. But she had set a goal to become a teacher and decided to allow nothing to interfere with her quest for knowledge. Not even poetry, for she had put it aside to focus on her studies. If God wanted her to write poems, He would show her the way and grant her the time. Until then, she would feed her mind with knowledge.

—3—

Teacher and Poet

*F*or six years Fanny abstained from writing poetry. As she studied, rhymes danced through her thoughts like butterflies on a bed of sunflowers, but she fought them off. Arithmetic continued to give her trouble, but she quite naturally excelled in subjects such as grammar, rhetoric and history, where there were no numbers, tables or rules to remember. Dr. Russ had excused her from arithmetic, but Dr. Jones put her back in the class with threats that he would keep her there until she learned it. With arithmetic back in her life, Fanny realized that she would never win a teaching post at the Institute until she mastered the "monster."

During these difficult learning years, Fanny remembered "one restless, witching little sprite that kept creeping up to me by night and day, and inviting me to take trips with her into the unknown; and the name of that sprite was Poetry. She was ever tugging away at my hands, or my hair, or my heartstrings, and whispering, 'Sister Fanny, come with me.'"

When she could no longer drive away the "sprite," Fanny took her problem to Dr. Jones, to whom she had pledged rigid concentration on her studies. The superintendent listened to her pleas kindly and thoughtfully. Having made her appeal, Fanny rested her case, but Dr. Jones suddenly changed his mind and said, "There are a great many people who write rhymes because they are poetry lovers rather than poets." He left Fanny with the impression that she might be of the "poetry lover" variety, but what he really wanted was for her to master arithmetic. He made Fanny promise to give poetry no more thought for three months.

"I did not like it one little bit," she recalled, "but I believed the superintendent knew what was best for me and religiously avoided a rhyme as I would the measles."

In God's sight, everyone has a special place, and Fanny began to wonder if her youth had been misspent on poems. She believed that Dr. Jones intended to "cure" her of the compulsion to write rhymes as if it were a dangerous disease. She had almost attained enough skill in grammar, rhetoric, and history to teach at the Institute, and she feared that by defying Jones, he would never put her on the staff. For three months she blocked out rhymes, and much to her surprise, arithmetic suddenly began to make sense. In her heart, however, she believed that even if she mastered the "monster," Jones would find some other reason to discourage her from wasting time on poems. But the Lord took a special interest in Fanny's plight, and in His own time led Dr. George Combe on a visit to the Institute.

Dr. Combe, a distinguished scientist who came from Scotland, specialized in the study of phrenology. He had written many papers on the subject and believed that he could determine a person's mental capacity and aptitude by the shape of one's head. He quite naturally developed an interest in the students at the Institute because they were all blind. With the superintendent's approval, Dr. Combe chose several students for examination—among them, Fanny.

She sat patiently and waited as the learned doctor ran his hands over the heads of the boys, carefully feeling the contours. When he came to a little fellow, he paused for a moment and said, "Why, here is a splendid mathematician!" Then, after a few more rubs, he exclaimed, "Amazing! Why this boy can do anything in mathematics."

The test group suddenly took notice, for Dr. Combe was absolutely right. The lad could put numbers together as fast as a modern computer. He could perform feats of division and multiplication a moment after the numbers were given to him. Fanny sat sullenly on the sidelines, a little envious that God had granted such power to the boy while for so many years she had struggled with simple addition and subtraction.

When Dr. Combe said, "Now for the girls," Fanny felt a little tremble as she heard him approach. Then she felt his hands moving gently to her head, first on it, then around it—a little squeeze here, another somewhere else. She felt a wild impulse to run. Barely a sound came from the filled room. The suspense became unendurable as Fanny felt his warm, searching hands move to her temples. And then the miraculous verdict came.

"Why! Here is a poet!" Dr. Combe declared. Fanny could not see the doctor as he turned to the superintendent, but she clearly heard the words: "Give her every advantage that she can have; let her hear the best books and converse with the best writers, and she will make her mark in the world."

At the words of Dr. Combe, Fanny could have fallen from her chair. She could not see the reaction of Dr. Jones, but she suspected he would disapprove. The following morning he

summoned her to his office. Fanny expected
another thoughtful lecture on why she should
pursue some other course in life. Instead, Dr.
Jones greeted her warmly and said, "Fanny, you
may write all the poetry you want."

Not only did Dr. Jones encourage her, he
provided instruction in how lines should rhyme.
He assigned special teachers to her and instructed
them to "make Fanny Crosby a first-class writer."

For this wonderful, sudden, happy change
in her life, she thanked God for bringing Dr.
Combe, who stayed but one day at the institution. Phrenology, the Scottish doctor's specialty,
became a rage in the nineteenth century, and
some practitioners used it to determine such
things as whether a person possessed a criminal
mind. As a science, phrenology soon lost cred-
ibility. Some scientists, however, have special
gifts, and Dr. Combe may have been one of them.
He made no mistake when he singled out the
little mathematician and the aspiring poet.

"I was taught all the intricacies of verse,"
Fanny recalled, "until I began to wonder that
the subject which I thought a very simple, easy
sort of thing had so many complications. I learned
to analyze, to parse, to scan, to write in different
measures, and I began to worry lest I should dis-
appoint the high expectations that Dr. Combe

had raised."

During this time, God granted Fanny another gift. In 1842 she passed her twenty-second birthday, and Dr. Jones, who had become her solid supporter, put her on the staff of the Institute to teach grammar, rhetoric, and history. "What a pleasure it was," Fanny recalled, "to know that I was imparting to others the same blessings of knowledge for which I had so longed through so many days and nights."

But even as a teacher, Fanny Crosby was still a student. She carried the title of the Institute's "Poet Laureate," but soon began to realize how little she knew of her honorable title. Dr. Jones brought in a gentleman named Hamilton Murray, who admitted that he could not write poetry but could teach it. He had a poetic temperament, a fine rich voice, but very few students—none of whom interested him as much as Fanny. For hours on end he would sit with her and read poems written by the world's masters, and even one of America's best, William Cullen Bryant. Murray believed in a certain amount of imitation and encouraged Fanny to practice by using the masters' styles. He pointed out her defects and guided her in making corrections. Eventually they parted ways, not because Fanny no longer needed instruction, but because Mr. Murray needed to earn a living.

"With rare faithfulness, and much kindness, considering that his pupil was not a rich man's daughter but a poor blind girl just starting out in life, he toiled for my benefit," Fanny said, "and though I could not pay him in money, he had my heartfelt gratitude."

God seemed to lead one phase of Fanny's life into another with barely a pause in between. The Institute had a fine little orchestra, and each year it seemed to get better. The idea of putting words to music or music to words intrigued Fanny, but the process baffled her. To her, poetry was the music of words alone, but when matched with notes, as in hymns, the combination gave great praise to the Lord. She could strum the guitar or finger the piano and sing her verses right along with the notes, but she could not write music and fretted over the handicap. She prayed to God for help, and in 1843 the answer came in an unexpected manner. Dr. Jones announced that William Cullen Bryant planned to come to the Institute to hear a concert. The Lord was opening the world to Fanny in other ways—words to music could wait.

The Institute's staff made careful preparations for Bryant's visit, including a grand reception. Fanny attended as a teacher, and as Bryant proceeded down the row of greeters, he came to her. She admitted that "little timid I never expected more than a conventional greeting, as I was a total stranger. To my surprise, he gave me a warm grasp of the hand, commented upon my poor little rhythmical efforts, commended them in a tone sincere, and told me to go on bravely with my work. He never knew how much good he did by those few words to the young girl that had hardly hoped to touch the hem of his proud robe of poetic genius."

Such inspiration became the tonic of life for her as she struggled with blindness. If Fanny Crosby ever faltered in her quest to conquer her world of darkness, the great men and women who touched her life gave her hope and determination whenever she felt burdened by her handicap. They all seemed to come from God at an important moment of need in her life.

Then in 1844 came Horace Greeley, the young founder of the *New York Tribune*—and it seemed the Lord had flung open another door. At first, Fanny thought the country made "a queer mistake by honoring him" as a great man, but on the occasion of a second meeting, she changed her mind. He spoke with such intelligence on history, literature, and social ethics that Fanny decided he must be pretty smart after all. Shortly, to her surprise, Greeley asked her to recite some of her poems. Fanny accepted the invitation, and her favorite verses flowed like music from her lips.

"They are wonderful," Greeley said with applause. "Perhaps you would write some poems for the *Tribune*."

"I would be delighted," Fanny replied.

When the reception ended, she hurried back to her room to begin work. "I was so proud," she confessed, "at having been recognized as a poet by such a great genius as Horace Greeley."

A short time later, Fanny's first published poems appeared in the widely circulated *New York Tribune*. The event became a great moment in her life. At the age of twenty-four, she had reached another milestone—one that started as a tiny pebble tossed in the brook that flowed behind the cottage where God had given her life. Without the loving care and guidance of Grandmother Crosby, Fanny might never have heard the quiet splash, the singing ripples of the brook, the gurgle of cold water rushing over her feet, or the screech of the kingfisher peering into the depths for its morning meal. So on the eighty-second birthday of her beloved grandmother, Fanny wrote:

How pleasant to look on a brow like hers,
   With hardly a trace of care;
How cheerful the light of her beaming eye,
   As she sits in her easy chair.

So little the change in her dear, kind face
   We scarce can believe its true
That she numbers today her four-score
      years,
   Her four-score years and two.

Her winter of age, though the snowflakes
      fell,
   Has never been dark nor drear,
She moves with the vigor of younger feet,
   And her mind is bright and clear.

She merrily talks of the olden time,
   Of friends in youth she knew;
She is sprightly and gay, though she
      numbers today,
   Her four-score years and two.

And now as we come with our birthday
      gifts,
   When she views them o'er and o'er,
And the earnest "God bless you, my
      children dear,"
   Is breathed from her lips once more,

We think how devoted our mother's love,
What a sunshine of joy she gives,
And we feel as we tenderly kiss her cheek,
What a comfort that she still lives.

A letter for Fanny arrived at the Institute
from her grandfather. He had walked four miles
to buy a copy of the *Tribune*—just to obtain his
granddaughter's poem. When he returned home
and read the verses, pride filled his heart, so he
wrote Fanny that he had been "well paid for his
trouble." The note from Grandfather Crosby
meant more to her than the poem in the paper.
She remembered his words from long ago, when
she was a child and he had said, "We indeed
have a poet in the family, and . . . she will be an
honor to the whole family."

Anybody reading Fanny's verses would find
it hard to believe that she had been blind almost from birth. She seemed to see her
grandmother's brow, her beaming eye, her old
rocking chair, snowflakes falling, and the sunshine of joy on her dear, kind face—all images
that required sight. It was also Fanny's way of
thanking the person who, with God's guidance,
had given her a very special kind of sight.

As teacher and poet, Fanny's life was about
to change in many ways. God had nursed her

along slowly, always leading her towards Him. But the Lord wanted Fanny to have a full life, one which expanded her senses, so He nudged her into the humming world swirling all about her.

— 4 —

Reaching Out

*I*n 1837 workers laid the cornerstone for a grand new building to house the Institute for the Blind. As on most large, impressive structures made of stone—especially those of three stories—work progressed slowly. By 1843, one hundred and fifty students—all blind—filled the finished dormitory. Because the new Institute had been financed by the state, the government took an interest in their new creation, and officials stopped often for a tour. Schools for the blind were not so common then, and, Fanny noted, "We were quite objects of curiosity."

Fanny's poems now appeared in many of New York's papers, and visitors to the Institute often asked for her to be their tour guide. "It was little blind me leading those that were not blind," Fanny recalled, "but I knew every inch of the establishment almost as well as if I could see."

When Fanny grew tired of answering the same old questions asked by sightseers, she gave the chore to some of the brighter students. One lad, who had just finished guiding a large group through the rooms and halls, told Fanny that the guests had asked how blind people managed to find their mouths while eating.

"What did you tell them?" she asked.

"I informed them," said the blind boy gravely, "that we hitched one end of a string to the leg of our chair, and the other to our tongue, and by that means managed to prevent the food from losing its way."

Teachers scolded the lad for his rude remark, but they privately laughed about it many times afterward.

In 1825 Governor DeWitt Clinton of New York had opened the Erie Canal. The great ditch stretched across the state and at Albany connected the Hudson River to Lake Erie. In 1843, with funds from the state treasury, the canal operators made a flatboat available to the Institute, along with a captain, a mule driver, and a maid. When Fanny and her blind companions stepped on board, the crew met them coldly. They wondered what pleasure sightless people would get from a scenic tour.

"Five minutes after we got on board," Fanny related, "the captain found that we were inclined to enjoy life with an abundance of innocent amusement."

When they got under way, the captain

took Fanny aside and said, "Well, you folks are the jolliest crew I ever shipped. To tell the truth," he added, "I dreaded this trip and expected to strike a sort of funeral procession the whole length of the big ditch, but I guess it's going to be a circus all the way, and a good one."

What began as a "circus" had its sober moments as the boat passed through the hill regions. None of the beautiful scenery could be seen by the passengers, but its presence could be felt. The warm touch of the sun, the fragrance of wildflowers, and the earthy smell of livestock all brought back Fanny's memories of childhood. She heard the cheery hail of boatmen passing and felt the fresh sweep of country borne by the wind. There were stops at Schenectady, Utica, Rome, Syracuse, and Rochester, where the students and teachers went ashore to entertain the public. Fanny recited her poems to audiences of hundreds, and local orchestras turned out with their instruments to accompany the Institute's singers.

"With God's blessing," she said, "we made a pretty good show and were always overwhelmed with praises and invitations to come again." Because the purpose of the tour was to rouse the public's interest in educating the blind, "we usually netted a nice little sum for the Institute."

In many of the towns where Fanny stopped, mothers of sightless children came forward seeking help. She found it hard to turn them away, but those moments revealed to her the need for more schools to educate the blind. Fanny made a pledge to herself to give them help, and though she had no money or influence, she vowed to help them get an education.

A side trip to Oswego brought Fanny a gift that would not be fulfilled for fifteen years. A local mother, Mary Van Alstyne, became so impressed by the work of the Institute that she resolved to send her blind son there. She approached Fanny with the boy, and with tears in her eyes, said, "Miss Crosby, when Alexander arrives, please take good care of him." Fanny promised, never realizing that the boy would one day become her husband.

The tour continued on to one of the great wonders of the world—Niagara Falls.

"But what can you see of the Falls?" someone asked.

"Much more than you would suppose," Fanny replied. "Seeing is not all done with the optic organs."

From classes taught at the Institute, everybody in the group knew of the immense chasm where the waters of four Great Lakes plunged one hundred and sixty-four feet into the rocks below. "We had seen it over and over again in our imaginations," Fanny recalled, "but nothing could replace being there, in its presence. I could almost fancy I heard the morning stars singing together, and the sons of God shouting for joy."

For a poet, just being at the Falls became a spiritual experience. Her limbs felt the great surge of waters rumbling into a cataract where it plunged and threw up a spray that washed across her face. When she learned of the rainbow in the mist, her thoughts wandered back to the day on the hill when her grandmother described the delicate colors of God's heavenly arch. She stood with her friends atop Table Rock—which in years to come would be swept into froth below—then lingered by the swirling whirlpool and imagined being drawn into its mighty vortex.

"It was all a little frightening," Fanny said, "the trumpet voice of this king of cataracts proclaiming the power of the Almighty hand."

After the trip ended, the group got together to discuss their impressions. "The blind see more than those with sight," Fanny decided, "because they get descriptions from different points of view that are not necessary to give to people who can look for themselves."

For Fanny, tours were only beginning. She

had made a pledge to help the blind, and in 1844, when the managers of the Institute formed a party to go to Washington, they asked her to join it. The reason soon became clear. They wanted Congress to pass legislation creating more schools for the blind and providing free education to sightless children in every state of the Union. At that point Fanny learned of the great importance the superintendent placed upon her presentation.

When asked to recite a poem before the House and Senate, she had, at the age of twenty-four, "one of the most distinguished audiences of her life." Being the first poet ever invited to speak before Congress jarred her nerves but not her message. When she finished reciting a thirteen-stanza poem, the chamber erupted in a thunder of applause so loud that it startled her. Shouts went up for an encore. She stood before them, waiting for silence, and chose an elegy she had written on the sudden death of Hugh Legare, President John Tyler's former secretary of war. By the time Fanny finished, she had Congress in tears. When the performance ended, Legare's sister met Fanny as she left the chamber and gave her a beautiful family ring.

During the reception that followed, distinguished men came before her—some whose names had already become a part of the nation's rich history. Both John Quincy Adams, the sixth president of the United States, and Senator James Buchanan, who would become the fifteenth president, greeted her warmly. From the House of Representatives came a humble, self-educated man, Andrew Johnson, who would be the seventeenth president. And there was Hannibal Hamlin, who later was Abraham Lincoln's vice-president, and Stephen A. Douglas, Honest Abe's able political opponent from Illinois. Among others who greeted her during the reception was Jefferson Davis, who in 1861 became the first and only president of the Confederacy, and Alexander Stephens, his vice-president. At every opportunity, Fanny spoke of the needs of blind children she had met on the trip across New York State, always adding, "and there must be so many more."

When the trip ended, the superintendent considered it a great success, but no funds came from Congress—not for the institution or for anyone. If the great men of Washington would do nothing for the blind, then Fanny would take on the job herself. She taught no classes that spring, and to raise money for the Institute she concentrated on publishing her first book of poems, titled *The Blind Girl and Other Poems*.

Her old teacher, Hamilton Murray, wrote the preface and asked the public for small donations. He even suggested that the authoress was in ill health and needed funds. At the time, Fanny was not well, but the photograph that appeared on the cover of the book showed a healthy young woman about four feet nine inches tall and weighing one hundred pounds. The title, *The Blind Girl . . .* , came from the first poem of her book. The first stanzas described her own birthplace:

> Her home was near an ancient wood,
> Where many an oak gigantic stood,
> And fragrant flowers of lovely hue
> In that sequestered valley grew.
>
> A church there reared its little spire,
> And in their neat and plain attire,
> The humble farmers would repair
> On Sabbath morn to worship there.

In the poem she also spoke of her playmates:

> With their laugh the woodland rang,
> Or if some rustic air they sang,
> These rural notes of music sweet
> The woodland echoes would repeat.

After the book went into print, the Institute bought a bundle of copies to sell to visitors. One afternoon, as Fanny showed a gentleman through the school, he spied the stack. "Oh, here is the Fanny Crosby book," he said with mounting interest. "You must know her, I suppose."

Fanny merely nodded, and knowing that her picture was on the cover, she kept her silence.

While paying for a copy, he asked, "Is she a likable girl?"

"Oh, no!" Fanny replied with a shake of her head. "Far from it!"

The buyer gave Fanny his card and departed. She later learned that her visitor, Johann Ludwig Tellkampf, was an eminent professor at Columbia College.

Fanny's book of poems became a popular item in New York and found its way into many homes in New England. Had her grandfather lived to see the book in print, he would have gone to the grave a proud man. He died a few months too soon and lay at rest in the country churchyard at Doanesburg.

Since childhood, Fanny had been impressed by the great hymns sung each Sunday in church. At times she tried to combine her own poems with music. When writing *The Blind Girl* she added "An Evening Hymn," and though she never thought of it as her first hymn, it was.

Her health declined during the long hours she toiled when writing her first book, and late that summer Dr. J. W. G. Clements of the Institute sent her home to recuperate. She found the household in some turmoil. Her stepfather, Thomas Morris, had abandoned her mother to join Joseph Smith and the Mormons in Illinois. He took with him his two daughters, but fifteen-year-old William refused to go and remained at home with Mercy. Carrie was still a baby and Julia a busy three-year-old. Fanny enjoyed being with her family and helping her mother. Morris eventually followed the Mormons to Utah and died there as Brigham Young's gardener.

In September Fanny returned to New York in perfect health. To her surprise, Alexander Van Alstyne, the blind boy she had met at Oswego, greeted her. Fanny remembered her pledge to Mrs. Van Alstyne and took the boy under her personal care. For the next four years he attended several of her classes and, though a student, became almost a constant companion. In 1848 he graduated and went off to Union College in Schenectady, but he would soon be back as more than just an instructor.

Though *The Blind Girl* sold well, the income from the little book could never cover the financial needs of the school. So in 1846 Fanny joined another delegation to Congress. This one included members from institutes for the blind in Philadelphia and Boston. Once again the group sought funds for more tuition-free schools. Fanny dedicated and sang a song to President James Polk, who had just declared war on Mexico. Once again she made a hit, and during the reception that followed she spoke with many of the same men she had met in 1844. "While I could not see these brilliant men," said Fanny, "I could feel their kindness, their appreciation, and their sympathy." But with the government's money going to the war, not a penny more went to schools for the blind.

Fanny tired of being asked to write poems for every occasion that involved the school, but she considered it an obligation. Her toil and talent attracted funds, and the new superintendent, James Chamberlain, was forever asking her to write "something nice" for every important visitor. She preferred earning money by publishing her poetry in Horace Greeley's *New York Tribune*, James G. Bennett's *New York Herald*, or the *Saturday Emporium* and the *Saturday Evening Post*. Elegies like "Weep Not for the Dead," written in 1848 on the death of John Quincy Adams, brought more money to the school than doodles for unimportant guests.

However, her poems, even those written without funds in mind, reached out and gave comfort to people. Men like the great Senator Henry Clay would forever remember her verses. When Fanny learned that young Henry Clay, Jr., had been killed in Mexico, she wrote the beautiful elegy "On the Death of Colonel Clay." Much to her surprise six months later, the superintendent said the senator wished to visit the school and asked Fanny to write a poem. When Clay arrived, Fanny read her poem, and a reporter from the *Herald* noted that the senator seemed "much affected." Clay then led Fanny to the speaker's platform, where he turned to the audience and said, "This is not the only poem for which I am indebted to this lady. Six months ago, she sent me some lines on the death of my dear son."

"Then," Fanny recalled, "he did not speak for some minutes, while both of us stood there, weeping."

Two weeks later General Winfield Scott, the hero of the Mexican War, visited the school and spent a quiet hour with Fanny. They discussed her many patriotic poems, but much to Fanny's surprise, she discovered that Scott did not actually like war.

"How did it seem when you really found yourself in the halls of Montezuma?" she asked. "Did you feel like shouting?"

"No," the general growled, "I felt like falling on my knees and thanking God for the victory. War is a terrible thing—demoralizing, degrading, cruel, and devastating in all its effects."

The general's comments affected Fanny. She had developed a fascination for war from studying the Old Testament. Hereafter, she would think of wars differently.

The war had also been hard on President Polk. In ill health during the summer of 1848, he made arrangements for a quiet rest at the Institute. Since Fanny and Polk had met on past occasions, Superintendent Chamberlain asked her to look after him. Polk and the poetess walked and talked as old friends. But neither the President of the United States, the greatest living general, or all the members of Congress could impress Fanny. She truly loved her blind friends and her special relationship with God. And no official, whether an aide or the president himself, ever departed from the Institute without a small scolding from Fanny for not providing more funds to help the blind.

She had reached out to others, giving of

herself, and worked with all her strength to promote schools for the blind. But having given comfort to great men and sightless children, she was not prepared for what happened next.

—5—

Now She Belonged to Him

*D*uring the latter part of 1846, rumors reached the Institute of a great plague spreading across Russia and into Persia and India. Hundreds of thousands died, and by the spring of 1847 the epidemic reached Great Britain and took another 70,000 lives. A ship carrying English passengers brought the disease to New Orleans, and in a few weeks 3,500 died.

Word quickly spread to New York that cholera had come to the United States. There seemed to be no way to stop its spread once it established a foothold. "The news cast a very sober feeling over our little band of students," Fanny recalled, "and many became terrified." To those in fear, she gave comfort, promising that "God would do all things best for us, both in this world and the next.... And so we prayed," she said, "and waited."

During December of 1848, a packet ship from Havre landed at Staten Island bearing several persons suffering from cholera. A few weeks later, three people died in New York. Health officials made every effort to keep the disease from spreading, but the epidemic that began in New Orleans worked up the Mississippi River, taking lives in Memphis, St. Louis, Cincinnati, and Chicago. By May 1849, cholera entered New York with a vengeance, and, as Fanny said, "Its reign of terror was at hand."

Superintendent Chamberlain attempted to protect the students by sending them home. Most of the children lived in the country, where the disease was less likely to strike, but many of the children could not go home and remained at the Institute. Fanny also stayed, acting as Dr. Clements's nurse. "I was convinced that God would take care of us," she declared, "and that we could be of some help."

At first she occupied her time making cholera pills, but by mid-July more than five hundred persons were dying each week in Manhattan. As the epidemic spread, health officials in New York turned a school one block from the Institute into a cholera hospital and began filling it with the sick. The pestilence quickly infested the Institute and ten students died.

"The horrors of the situation grew upon us day by day," Fanny said. Many years later she could still recall the harsh call of the truckman, who stopped at the entrance to the Institute and hollered, "Bring out your dead!"

Fanny began to work among the dying at the nearby hospital, feeling her way from room to room. Nothing ever remained in the same place. Several times each day she stumbled over coffins which had been shoved into the hallway to be picked up and delivered to the truckman.

During the height of the epidemic an Irish priest, Father Theobald Mathew, arrived at the Institute for an untimely visit. To honor the occasion, the superintendent asked Fanny to write a poem. Though well known for his crusade against alcoholism, it was also believed that Father Mathew could perform miracles of healing. Fanny took time away from the hospital and wrote the poem, much to the delight of Father Mathew. For several days he followed Fanny about the hospital "like the visit of an angel to the house of Death" and was impressed by her great piety. When he left, he laid his hands upon her head and blessed her.

"His touch seemed to me," said Fanny, "like that of a saint who had been permitted to leave his abode in heaven for one single moment to cheer the desolate children of earth."

Fanny, though raised as a Presbyterian, found great comfort in Father Mathew, and through him acquired a lifelong love and respect for the Roman Catholic Church.

During all the terrible weeks of summer, Fanny toiled at the hospital, giving little thought to her own health. Once, when feverish, she believed herself in the grip of cholera. She swallowed a few pills and went to bed. In the morning she felt better, but when the superintendent discovered she had been ill, he ordered her to take a vacation. Fanny went home to Bridgeport and remained there until fall. When the freezes of November struck New York, the epidemic ceased. School resumed once more, but for Fanny life had become a bitter time of mourning. Too many of her precious students had been swept away by pestilence, and she kept asking herself, "Why? Why? Why?"

Fanny suffered from no particular disease, but for many months remained sad and depressed. She struggled to find or understand her eternal destiny. Had cholera taken her life, would she have been ready to meet God? Had she used her life to serve Him, or had she merely served her own interests? After experiencing so much death, she began to question her faith—not faith in God the Father and Jesus Christ—but faith in herself. She fretted over her life—not her blindness, but whether she had too lightly taken Dr. Jones's warning to not let success go to her head.

She even questioned her fame as "The Blind Girl," asking, "What does it mean in the face of death?"

To distract her thoughts, she began another book of poetry—*Monterey and Other Poems*—but the work progressed slowly. The effort was there but not the inspiration, so the verses came slowly. She taught only a few classes in 1850, but whenever she could get away on Sundays she attended the Methodist Broadway Tabernacle on 30th Street. She found the services warm, lively, and spiritual—not like the stern and solemn Presbyterian church of her youth.

For many years, an elder from the Eighteenth Street Methodist Church visited the Institute on Thursday evenings to bring the Word of God to the students. They met informally to sing, pray, read Scripture, and "testify" about the Lord. At first, Methodists seemed a little strange to Fanny. She provided the worshipers with music, but with the understanding that "they should not call upon me to speak or to testify." After the shock of seeing so many children killed by cholera, Fanny could not open her heart to God.

When Theodore Camp, a teacher at the Institute, invited Fanny to attend revivals at the Broadway Tabernacle, she declined. Camp kept the invitation open, and Fanny kept refusing—until after the night when she had a very strange dream. A visionary figure came to her and said, "Mr. Camp would like to see you." In her dream, Fanny entered the room and found him very sick and preparing to die.

"Fanny," he asked, "can you give up our friendship?"

"No, I cannot," she replied. "You have been my advisor and friend, and what could I do without your aid?"

"But," he replied, "why would you chain a spirit to earth when it longs to fly away and be at rest?"

"Well," Fanny said, "I cannot give you up of myself, but I will seek divine assistance."

"But will you meet me in heaven?"

Thinking those were her friend's last words, Fanny cried, "Yes, I will, God helping me."

Camp closed his eyes, but then suddenly opened them again, saying, "Remember, you promised a dying man."

Next, in Fanny's dream, the clouds seemed to roll away, and she awoke with a start. The words—Will you meet me in heaven?—lingered in her mind. Although her friend was in perfect health, she wondered whether her faith was really strong enough for her to meet Ted Camp in heaven—or any of her friends, if called to do so. She began to attend nightly meetings at the Thirteenth Street Methodist Church, and on two occasions sought peace with others at the altar. The assurance and joy she craved did not unfold until the night of November 20, 1850, when Fanny went to the altar alone. A prayer was offered, and spontaneously the congregation began to sing the grand old consecration hymn:

> Alas, and did my Saviour bleed?
> And did my Sovereign die?

When the singers reached the fifth and last verse—"Here, Lord, I give myself away, / 'Tis all that I can do"—Fanny felt suddenly "flooded with a celestial light." She sprang to her feet, shouting, "Hallelujah!" and for the first time in her life Fanny Crosby realized that "she had been trying to hold the world in one hand and the Lord in the other." Now she could take Him into both hands and fully into her heart and let Him lead her down the path of life.

On Thursday evening, when the Methodist elder came to the Institute, Fanny gave her first testimony at the meeting of the class. And when the old pride of hearing her own voice crept into her thoughts, she resolved to testify again and again until she drove out the demon of self-praise.

For several weeks she struggled with the problem, because she believed that giving her life to God meant a complete surrender of her will. Fanny had always been a deeply religious woman, but she felt something immensely lacking in her spiritual life. With doubts still present, she prayed, promising "to do my duty whenever the dear Lord should make it plain to me."

The Lord did not keep Fanny waiting. A session or two later, the visiting Methodist elder asked her to close the class meeting with a brief prayer. Fanny's first thought was "I can't"; then her voice of conscience whispered, "But your promise . . ." "From that moment," she said, "I have never refused to pray or speak in a public service, with the result that I have been richly blessed."

Fanny never forgot that spirit-filled moment on November 20, 1850, when she knelt at the altar of the Thirteenth Street Methodist Church and felt flooded by God's "celestial light." For thirty years she had carried a burden of doubt, never confident of her mission. Then, in an instant, the Lord revealed Himself and thrust off the anchor weighing on Fanny's soul. During her life she wrote many poems to celebrate that moment, among them "I See the Light":

> I see the Light, 'tis coming,
>   It breaks upon my soul;
> It streams above the tempest,
>   And ocean waves that roll.
>
> From skies with clouds o'ershadowed,
>   The mist dissolves away,
> I see the Light that leadeth,
>   To everlasting day.
>
> With joy no words can utter,
>   My heart is all aglow,
> I see the Light of Glory,
>   Now let the anchor go.

On that night in November, all the clouds that had clung to Fanny's soul since the days of the cholera plague were lifted. For the United States, the epidemic had lasted about six months. For Fanny, the effects had continued for another year. She realized that God had placed her among the sick and, when the fever struck her down during the summer of 1849, that the Lord had intervened and made her well. Now she belonged to Him, and she would never look back.

—6—

"There's Music in the Air"

*D*uring the early 1850s, Fanny continued her work at the New York Institute for the Blind and at the age of thirty-one published her second book of verse—*Monterey and Other Poems*. Some of the poems revealed her depressed state of mind during the months following the cholera epidemic. But the later verses were filled with references to the Spirit of God, as He had blessed her with His light and filled her heart with joy. Fanny felt as though she had been thrust upon another journey but had not mapped out the means of travel.

She remained at the Institute, entertaining guests and raising money for the school. When the famous Swedish singer Jenny Lind came to America, one of the first places she stopped was the Institute. The students assembled to hear her sing, and her voice filled the chamber with the most marvelous music. When the concert ended, Fanny recited a short poem that deeply touched Miss Lind. The first and last stanzas read:

We ask no more why strains like thine
Enchant a listening throng,
For we have felt in one sweet hour
The magic of thy song.
Yet, Sweden's daughter, thou shalt live
In every grateful heart;
And may the choicest gifts of heaven
Be thine, where'er thou art.

For Jenny Lind's first concert in America, given in New York City, she received $10,000. She immediately donated the entire sum to charity.

Fanny's reputation at the Institute continued to grow, and the new superintendent, T. Colden Cooper, made her dean of students. In the fall of 1853 he hired a young man named William Cleveland to head the school's literary department. A few months later, William hired his sixteen-year-old brother, Grover, to teach reading, writing, and arithmetic. When not teaching, Grover served as Superintendent Cooper's clerk. The Clevelands' father had died recently, and William, knowing of Fanny's ability to give comfort and sympathy, asked her help. "Grover has taken our father's death very much to heart," he told her, "and I wish you would go into the office and talk to him once in a while."

So Fanny did.

Grover stood six feet tall and seemed like a giant to Fanny, but she soon won his confidence. He loved poetry, and they quickly became great friends—so much so that Grover ignored his clerical chores to spend more of his time with Fanny. They would sit together in the clerk's office, she composing verses and he writing them down. At times they would just chat and have a good time together.

Cooper, whom Fanny privately called a "cruel incompetent," did not think his clerk should be wasting time copying poems. When his angry glances—which Fanny could not see— failed to discourage Grover, the superintendent one day stormed into the clerk's office. "Miss Crosby," he growled, "when you want Mr. Cleveland to copy a piece for you, I will thank you to ask me. My clerks have other work to do than copy poetry!"

Having violated no rule, Fanny was dumbfounded by the unexpected assault. She could not decide whether to snap back or do the ladylike thing and cry. In the end, she did neither. After Cooper left the room, Grover touched her hand and said, "We are entirely within our rights, Fanny, and he had no business to interrupt us. Come tomorrow with another poem, and I will copy it for you." Then with a laugh he added, "I suppose Cooper will be back again. If he comes, and if I were you, I would give him a few paragraphs of plain prose—something that he would not very soon forget."

Fanny took Grover's advice and returned the next day with a poem to be copied. She also had decided upon "a few paragraphs of plain prose," so when Cooper stomped into the office to deliver another scolding, Fanny shot back: "I want to remind you that I am second to no one in this Institute aside from yourself, and I have lived with your insolence so long that I will do so no longer." She reminded Cooper that her poems had been used mainly to benefit the Institute and to call new students to the school. "If you ever refer to this matter again," she said, "I will ask the trustees what they think about it."

When Fanny met with Grover the following day, Cooper stayed away. "You will never have any trouble from him again," Grover predicted.

In 1885, and again in 1893, Fanny looked back upon these incidents with fond memories— for those were the years that Grover Cleveland became the 22nd and 24th President of the United States.

In 1854 the Cleveland brothers left the

Institute in disgust. Superintendent Cooper's practices had overcrowded the school. Children were no longer pupils but were treated like inmates at a penal asylum. Those years were difficult for Fanny, but her love for the children and devotion to the school kept her there. Had she not stayed, she might never have met George F. Root, who, like Grover Cleveland, would change her life—but in a different way.

In 1845 Root began to give music lessons at the Institute. He considered himself a composer of sorts, but he came and went and Fanny saw little of him when he was there. One day in 1854 she heard him playing a beautiful melody and, learning that he had just written it, said, "Oh, Mr. Root, why don't you publish that?"

Root, a small, bearded man, squinted at her with piercing eyes and replied, "I have no words for it and cannot purchase any."

"Ah," said Fanny. "Let me try." With barely a pause, she began, "Try this:

" O come to the greenwood, where nature is
    smiling,
Come to the greenwood, so lovely and gay,
There will soft music, thy spirit beguiling,
Tenderly carol thy sadness away."

Almost speechless, Root shouted, "They fit! They fit!" So he played the song once more and Fanny sang it.

"Will you write for me?" he asked hopefully.

Fanny agreed, but told Root that he would have to wait until summer because she too was busy with school. "In the meantime," she said, "I have hundreds of verses. Instead of me writing new lines for you, why don't you try to put music to ones I have already written?"

For three years Fanny worked with Root, and popular songs with an uplifting message filled the music hall at the school. "Rosalie, the Prairie Flower," "Glad to Get Home," "Proud World, Goodbye," and "There's Music in the Air" were set to notes by Root. Thousands of copies in sheet music and bound booklets crossed the country from New York to the concert halls of California. Together, George Root and Fanny composed more than fifty songs.

They also published cantatas—*The Flower Queen* and *The Pilgrim Fathers*—which were complex arrangements involving several instruments, a choir, and soloists. Root would usually develop the plot and hum a bit of the melody to get the rhythm. The very next day Fanny would have two or three poems ready. Root then selected the verses he liked best and composed the music. *The Flower Queen* became a big hit in the East. For *The Pilgrim Fathers*, another hit, Root worked on the musical score with Lowell Mason, but he never gave Fanny credit for the lyrics. He paid her a small sum for her verses while pocketing thousands of dollars for himself. Her work, however, eventually came to the attention of William B. Bradbury, who sometimes gave concerts at the Broadway Tabernacle. But ten more years passed before Bradbury finally met Fanny.

In the meantime, Fanny turned thirty-five and discovered a different kind of music in the air. She was still a spinster but admitted she "had a heart that was hungry for love." She often expressed her feelings and disappointment in her poems. But all that began to change in 1855 when Alexander Van Alstyne returned to the Institute as music instructor. "Van" had become the first of the school's students to enroll in a regular college, where he studied music, Greek, Latin, philosophy, and theology.

Though Van was eleven years younger than Fanny, their mutual interest in music and poetry drew them together. "We soon became very much concerned for each other," Fanny recalled. They both disliked the cruel manner in which Super-

intendent Cooper managed the Institute. He had
made her "happy home" a cheerless place where
teachers were underpaid and children were mis-
treated and poorly fed.

In the autumn of 1857, Van left the Institute, moved to Long Island, and began to tutor
students in music. Five months later Fanny, sadly
dissolving her long relationship with the Institute, joined him. On March 5, 1858, in the little
town of Maspeth on Long Island, they were qui-
etly married—the beginning of a life of deep
mutual devotion and love.

Away from the Institute, Fanny's life
changed drastically. Now a housewife and no
longer the center of attention, she lived with
her husband in a country village where nobody
knew her as a famous poet. She enjoyed the
change, for the country air revived her spirits
and gave her pleasure. She began work on a third
book of poems—*A Wreath of Columbia's Flowers*—while her husband, to raise extra cash, served
as a paid organist at several area churches. He
soon became known as one of New York's finest
organists and a master of the piano, cornet, and
other instruments. Though Fanny could not see
her husband's features, she learned that as he
played his face beamed with a spiritual light.

After their marriage Van insisted that

Fanny keep her literary name. Because they needed money, she rushed the completion of her third book of poetry and added three short stories. A *Wreath of Columbia's Flowers* should have been the best of her three books, but as Fanny admitted, "It suffered more than the others from the need of careful pruning and revision." The reasons were not clear, but as she worked on the book, she often put it aside to write a hymn. Van composed the music, and as they worked together Fanny began to feel God's hand drawing her toward a new career.

In 1859, tragedy struck the newlyweds. Fanny became a mother, but the child died in infancy. She experienced months of sorrow, feeling that a very special gift had been taken from her. Her grief continued, and she received no comfort from her country neighbors. She needed something to occupy her mind, more familiar ground to rekindle her spirit. So in 1860 Van took her back to Manhattan and rented a room not far from the Institute.

She could hardly believe how much the city had changed. New York had grown to 700,000 inhabitants, and it hummed with Christian revival. Some called it religion's Second Great Awakening. Missions sprouted up everywhere, "Sunday Schools" became popular, a great movement against slavery had begun, and groups everywhere were spreading the gospel of Jesus Christ. Fanny even discovered that her distant cousin, Dr. Howard Crosby, had become the young pastor at the Fourth Avenue Presbyterian Church and helped to organize the city's Young Men's Christian Association (YMCA). Churches flung open their doors each day at noon, and people came by the thousands to pray. Daily, twelve hundred Christians packed the John Street Methodist Church, and Fanny began to make regular visits to the Plymouth Congregational Church where the great Henry Ward Beecher preached.

In 1861, with the revival in full swing, the Civil War began. Fanny's sister, Julie, married Byron Atherton, and off he went to war. Her stepbrother, William Morris, joined and followed. Fanny was proud of her two brothers, and wherever she went she carried a small American flag. One evening she took it into a Manhattan restaurant with a group of friends. A Southern lady spied Fanny's silk flag and growled, "Take that dirty thing away!" Much to the surprise of her companions, Fanny sprang to her feet and started in the direction of the voice, warning, "Repeat that remark at your risk!" The owner of the restaurant broke up the fight before blows were exchanged.

Julie's husband received a wound in Virginia in 1863, and William became sick with tuberculosis. Both lived for many years but never again in good health. Nonetheless, Fanny remained a patriot and wrote many songs that were set to music by several composers. In the first stanza of the "Song to Jeff Davis," the President of the Confederacy, she wrote:

Come, thou vaunting boaster,
Jeff Davis and thy clan,
Our northern troops are waiting,
Now, show thyself a man.
Advance with all thy forces,
We dare thy traitor band,
We'll blow thy ranks to atoms!
We'll fight them hand to hand.

She ended the song with a rhyme suggesting that Jeff Davis's head be cut off, like that of all traitors. Then in the warlike "Union Song"—set to the music of many instruments—Fanny wrote:

Death to those whose impious hands,
Burst our Union's sacred bands,
Vengeance thunders, right demands—
Justice for the brave.

For a tiny woman weighing no more than one hundred pounds, Fanny Crosby's songs during the Civil War contained little of the sweetness and charity so present in her early works. Her pen became her sword—the only way she could fight the war. Her songs became rallying cries for the men in the field and for recruiting offices in the cities. Mild, gentle, loving Fanny Crosby had become a warrior!

With war's end in sight, she returned to the writing she loved so well. For many years she had listened to the hymns and Christian melodies in concerts given by William B. Bradbury. Fanny had never met the man, but in 1864 Reverend Peter Stryker, pastor of the Dutch Reformed Church on 23rd Street, suggested she pay him a visit. Once again, the Lord put her life back on course and changed it forever.

— 7 —

The Bradbury Years

In the 1860s, hymn writing began to change. The grave and solemn hymns of earlier years were giving way to new ones with radiant and spirited melodies. The old hymn writers seemed to write often about sin and hell. William Bradbury, who composed and arranged music, wanted people to praise God also and feel good about doing it. He could not get the type of verses he needed, and when Pastor Stryker introduced him to Fanny Crosby, he could not have been happier.

Bradbury, a very thin man with an enormous black beard, had been born in Maine fifty-four years earlier and studied music under Lowell Mason. He had helped introduce the organ into American churches, and—while working under Mason—he had adopted the music of European masters. Now his style began to change, favoring lighthearted melodies, simple to sing and easy to remember, like "Just As I Am," "He Leadeth Me," and "On Christ, the Solid Rock, I Stand."

During the interview Fanny could not see Bradbury, but she sensed that he was a good man and one she could trust. Like some blind persons, Fanny could size up an individual with uncanny accuracy. She immediately liked Bradbury, and he instantly liked her.

"Fanny," he said with gracious sincerity, "I thank God that we have at last met, for I think you can write hymns, and I have wanted for a long time to have a talk with you. I wish you would begin, right away."

Fanny promised to bring him some verses before the end of the week. "It now seemed to me as if the great work of my life had really begun," she recalled.

When Fanny wrote poetry, she often had visions. Since the death of her baby, however, they had ceased. Now, as she looked for inspiration to write her first hymn for William Bradbury, the visions came again. She seemed led by a spirit to a very bright star, being lifted from her earthly body and carried toward it. Up and up they went, past millions of other stars, until they came to a celestial river. "May I not go on?" Fanny asked the visionary figure. "Not now," the spirit replied. "You must return to the earth and do your work there, but before you go, I will have the gates opened a little way, so you can hear one burst of the eternal music."

Fanny listened and "soon there came chords of melody such as I never had supposed could exist anywhere. The very recollection of it thrills me." Forever after, whenever she needed inspiration, she thought of her journey through the heavens.

Three days later she returned to Bradbury's office with her first hymn. In the first two of four stanzas, she spoke of her vision:

> We are going, we are going
>   To a home beyond the skies,
> Where the fields are robed in beauty,
>   And the sunlight never dies.
>
> Where the fount of joy is flowing
>   In the valley green and fair,
> We shall dwell in love together—
>   There shall be no parting there.

Bradbury quickly set the verse to music and titled it "We Are Going." In a hymnal he later published, he changed the name to "Our Bright Home Above."

While the Civil War still raged, Bradbury wanted to publish a militant hymn. His musical composition baffled all his many verse writers, so while Fanny was in his office he played it three times. She counted the measure and departed with the music set in her mind. In the morning she returned but found Bradbury gone. A clerk agreed to play the music on the piano while Fanny sang the lyrics. The astonished pianist whooped, "How in the world did you manage to write that hymn? Nobody ever supposed that you, or any other mortal, could adapt words to that melody."

Bradbury came into the office and noticed that Fanny had changed the title slightly. He then looked over the hymn and heartily agreed with his clerk. She had more than passed his test. "Fanny," he said, "I am surprised beyond measure, and now let me say that as long as I have a publishing house, you will always have work."

The hymn became immensely popular during 1864, but when the war ended in 1865, Bradbury decided to set it aside. Fanny protested and composed a missionary hymn to the same tune. "There's a Cry from Macedonia" became instantly popular and for many years appeared in sheet music and in all of Bradbury's hymnals.

Fanny soon discovered that Bradbury owned a huge collection of music without verse. He also had stacks of music with lines from other writers whose words he did not like. For four years Fanny worked side by side with Bradbury, picking the tunes she liked best and setting words to his music. She often composed six or seven hymns a day. During those years, Bradbury published three volumes of hymns, every one of them containing from thirty to forty of Fanny's verses.

During their working relationship, Bradbury became ill with tuberculosis. In the autumn of 1867 he summoned her and said, "Knowing you has been very pleasant for me, but it will soon be over. I am going to be forever with the Lord, and I will await you on the bank of the river."

Fanny sat nearby and cried, "Must I lose a friendship that I have enjoyed so much?"

"No," he replied, "take up my lifework where I lay it down, and you will not need to lose a friendship, though I am going away from you. Rather, you can strengthen it by striving to carry out my ideals."

Fanny wiped the tears from her eyes and said she would. On January 7, 1868, William Bradbury passed away. At his funeral in Montclair, New Jersey, the choir sang from Fanny's first hymn: "We are going, we are going, / To a home beyond the skies, / Where the roses never wither, / And the sunlight never dies."

Bradbury had wanted it that way.

During the funeral Fanny wept at the casket. At solemn moments like this, she often experienced surges of divine encouragement. A clear, beautiful voice seemed to come from the congregation, saying, "Fanny, pick up the work where Mr. Bradbury leaves it; take your harp from the willow, and dry your tears." The voice startled her. Others claimed they had heard it, too, but no one could point to the speaker.

Fanny knew she could never pick up Bradbury's work by herself, and his death brought great sorrow. She had always lived in poverty, but during her four years with Bradbury, life had become a little easier—but not too much easier, because she gave to the poor everything but what little she needed for herself and Van! Bradbury had introduced her to other musicians and publishers, among them Philip Phillips of Cincinnati. In 1865 Phillips had sent Fanny forty titles and asked her to compose the words. At the time, Bradbury had said, "Go ahead," so Fanny wrote hymns for all forty. She sent them to Cincinnati all at one time, and in 1866 Phillips published many of them in a hymnal titled *The Singing Pilgrim*.

In 1864, when Bradbury said to Fanny, "As long as I have a publishing house, you will always have work," he meant to keep his promise even after death. Two partners, Sylvester Main and Lucius H. Biglow, acquired Bradbury's business in 1868—and with it, Fanny Crosby. The voice in the sanctuary who told Fanny to take the harp from the willow seemed by some miracle to have put it in her hands. In a way, the new company brought two old friends together. Thirty-five years before, soon after Mrs. Crosby moved to Ridgefield, Sylvester Main had been Fanny's friend and neighbor. At the age of sixteen he became a singing teacher and more recently he had become the choir director at the Norfolk Street Methodist Church in New York. He started into the publishing business in the early 1860s, met Fanny at Bradbury's office, and renewed the old friendship.

Lucius Biglow, a local merchant, had been in business for a number of years. Bradbury knew both Biglow and Main well, and before he died, he encouraged them to form a partnership and continue the work of Bradbury and Company. Because of his pledge to Fanny, Bradbury's motives went beyond extending his own work. Neither Biglow nor Main knew very much about the publishing business, so they left the work of producing hymns to the poets and musicians of the firm. Fanny quickly established herself as the

most prominent of the poets and, more than anyone else, set the style of hymns for the next fifty
years.

The other member of the new company
was Hubert P. Main, Sylvester's son. Fanny had
met him in 1866 at Bradbury's office and considered him a fine composer. His knowledge of
music for hymns was his greatest asset and would,
in the years to come, become most helpful to
Fanny in her work.

While working with Bradbury, Fanny and
Van moved to Varick Street on the Lower West
Side of New York. The tenement housed thirty-
three people. Fanny and Van occupied half of a
third-floor garret, which had no running water
or access to outside air. They could afford a better place to live, but Fanny believed that her
mission was to live among the poor and give
them help. For them she wrote such hopeful
hymns as:

> Pass me not, O gentle Saviour,
> Hear my humble cry;
> While on others Thou art calling,
> Do not pass me by.

When writing hymns for different publishers, Fanny used many pen names—like Ella Dale

and Lizzie Edwards, or even Charles Bruce and Frank Gould, and as many as a hundred more. Because of this, it became difficult to trace the number of hymns she wrote. By 1870, everybody writing Christian music knew the name of Fanny Crosby and wanted her hymns, but most of her work using the Crosby name went to Biglow and Main. She could dictate hymns faster than a dozen composers could write the music, and the extra cash coming from other publishers helped her and Van make ends meet.

In 1873, Sylvester Main died, and Lucius Biglow, the senior member of the firm, continued the business for thirty more years. Hubert Main became the junior partner, and for all those many years, Fanny recalled, "We never had the slightest misunderstanding."

While working for Biglow and Main, Fanny became known around the world and especially in England. Every European composer visiting New York stopped at Biglow and Main and many of them stayed for many weeks. All had heard of "The Blind Poetess" who had written so many marvelous hymns and wanted to meet her. Some of them brought their own unpublished music, and Fanny would prepare a few stanzas of verse—often signing it with one of her pen names. They were amazed at her ability to feel the music and the speed at which she could compose verse. For those who brought no music, Fanny would often write a hymn and let them compose the music later.

Fanny did most of her writing in her mind. She knew how to write, but her memory was so keen that she seldom found it necessary. Biglow and Main would often assign two clerks to copy her dictation. Fanny would recite two lines from one hymn to the first clerk, then two lines of another poem to a second clerk—and then go back to the first clerk with two more lines! Only rarely would she change a word, and when those hymns were finished, she would start again with another.

Everybody marveled at Fanny's ability to dictate one hymn after the other—and often two at a time—all from memory. But if they attempted to praise this special talent, she would scold them, saying gently that "God gives everyone memory, but most people with sight lose it through laziness."

When Bradbury was alive, he had encouraged Fanny to work with Rev. Dr. Robert Lowry. Unlike Bradbury, who wrote the music before selecting the verse, Lowry asked for the verse before writing the music. Fanny enjoyed working with Lowry because she did not feel restrained by the measure of the music when composing the verses. One of their first hymns, "All the Way My Saviour Leads Me," became one of their best, and is still sung in many churches today. Thirty years later, Dr. Lowry helped Fanny select her best poems and hymns for a book titled *Bells at Evening*, and it remains today as one of her finest collections.

William Bradbury introduced Fanny to many of the men with whom she would work for more than forty years. Those closest to her all died at the height of their composing. Next to the death of Bradbury, the loss of Dr. Lowry wrung her heart the most. Thirty years later, as he lay dying at his home in Plainfield, New Jersey, Fanny crossed the river in a ferry and paid him one last visit. They talked together for a long time, remembering all the years they had worked and studied together. Finally he said to her, "Fanny, I am going to join those who have gone before, for my work is now done."

At first, she could not speak. Taking his hand, she held it gently. They prayed together, long into the evening. Then Fanny departed, saying, "I thank you, Doctor Lowry, for all that you have done for me. Good night, until we meet again."

After the evening prayers, words of verse

flowed through Fanny's thoughts. It always happened that way. Sometimes the words came from
great happiness—this time they came from great
grief. So for her friend Dr. Lowry, she wrote:

> A little while to weep for those we cher-
> ish,
> As one by one they near the river's brink;
> A little while to catch their sweet assur-
> ance,
> That we in heaven shall find each missing
> link;
> A little while and then the glorious dawn-
> ing
> Of that fair morn beyond the swelling tide,
> When we shall wake and in our Saviour's
> likeness,
> Perfect and pure, we shall be satisfied.

During Fanny's years with Bradbury and
Company she also met Dr. William Howard
Doane—who had come to New York in search
of a hymn for a special anniversary at the Five
Points Mission. He reviewed lines from dozens
of writers and found none to his liking. When
Dr. Lowry learned of Doane's problem, he asked
Fanny to send him one of her poems. At the
time, Fanny had not met Doane, but she had

been working on a hymn titled "More Like Jesus" and sent it to him by a messenger boy. Doane was busy at the mission talking with Dr. Van Meter, so when the messenger arrived, Doane put the hymn aside. Later he read it and instantly became excited. He chased after the messenger boy but could not find him. All the rest of that day he made inquiries to learn where Fanny lived. Late that evening he knocked on her door, and asked, "Are you Fanny Crosby?"

"Yes," she replied, wondering about the identity of her visitor.

"How glad I am to find you," he said. "I have been trying to do so all day, and at last I have succeeded."

Doane introduced himself, and they talked for a while. "I must pay you for the hymn," he said, "which I was more than glad to receive."

As he bid her goodbye, he pressed into Fanny's hand what she thought was a two dollar bill. She was not certain of the amount so she asked him, "What is this?"

"Twenty dollars," he said.

"But I cannot take so much," Fanny protested.

"The Lord sent me that hymn," he replied, "and you shall have nothing less than twenty dollars for it."

Doane returned the following evening with a new title and asked Fanny if she could write a hymn for it. She agreed and started work right away.

In the meantime, Doane worked on the hymn "More Like Jesus," and the melody came to him at once. When Dr. Van Meter stopped by to ask whether a hymn had been found, Doane happily replied, "Yes, and wait till you hear it." Together they walked to the nearby church, where Van Meter agreed to pump the organ while Doane played and sang the hymn:

> More like Jesus would I be,
> Let my Saviour dwell with me;
> Fill my soul with peace and love,
> Make me gentle as a dove;
> More like Jesus as I go,
> Pilgrim, in this world below;
> Poor in spirit would I be—
> Let my Saviour dwell in me.

Halfway through the hymn, Van Meter broke into tears and forgot to pump the organ. Together they tried once more, and this time they got through the hymn. Van Meter came out from behind the organ, threw his arms around Doane's neck, and cried, "Doane, where did you get that?"

"From Fanny Crosby," he replied, "and I just this moment finished writing the music."

Fanny always thanked the Lord for the four years she had spent with William Bradbury. He had introduced her to many important people, such as Lucius Biglow, Sylvester Main, Philip Phillips, Dr. Lowry, and Dr. Doane, who then became her friends. When he died in 1868, he left her a legacy—to work for God, and to praise Him with song—and for another forty-six years, she never stopped.

—8—

Hymns for the Ages

*H*oward Doane and Fanny Crosby became friends for life. She liked his melodies, and though they sometimes had a flavor of march music, they were simple, catchy tunes—easy to play and easy to remember. Doane composed "Hail to the Chief" and "Columbia, the Gem of the Ocean," songs still played and sung across America. During Fanny's life there were no radios, televisions, or records, and few people could afford to buy a piano. Songs did not survive unless people liked them well enough to remember the words and music.

Doane was not a great composer, nor even a particularly good musician, but he was a good Christian businessman. During his lifetime he wrote the melody for 2,300 hymns—and for half of those, Fanny wrote the verses. She believed that every word came from the "blessed Holy Spirit," and she never began a hymn without first kneeling to pray and asking God for inspiration.

Doane was amazed one day when he stopped at her tiny apartment and said, "I have exactly forty minutes before I must meet a train to Cincinnati. I have a tune for you. See if it says anything to you. Perhaps you can commit it to memory and then compose a poem to match it."

He hummed a simple melody, and Fanny, hearing it but once, clapped her hands and replied, "Why, that tune says 'Safe in the Arms of Jesus.'" She said a little prayer and then told Doane to take up a pen and write down her words.

Safe in the arms of Jesus,
Safe on His gentle breast,
There, by His Love o'ershaded,
Sweetly my soul shall rest.
Hark! 'tis the voice of angels,
Borne in a song to me,
Over the fields of glory,
Over the jasper sea.

Amazed, Doane took the hymn, published it, and the words and music became an instant success. Three years later Biglow and Main included it in their hymnal, and many church choirs and congregations still sing it today.

Fanny had another gift. She could often sense when someone near her was troubled—even persons she had not met. Once while visiting Dr. Doane in Cincinnati she spoke before a large group of young men. As her talk came to an end, she was filled with a feeling that "some mother's boy" in the audience "must be rescued this night or not at all."

Fanny knew not why, but as she closed the service, she said, "If there is a dear boy here tonight who has wandered away from his mother's home and his mother's teaching, would you please come to me at the end of this service."

Moments later a young lad of eighteen approached her and said, "Did you mean me?"

"Yes," she replied, touching him gently.

"I had promised mother to meet her in heaven," said the lad, "but the way I have been living, I don't think that will be possible now."

Fanny took hold of the boy, told him to kneel, and then began to pray. Doane watched, noting a new light that seemed to fill the youth's eyes. The lad rose, filled with repentance, and said, "Now I can meet my mother in heaven, for I have found her God."

Earlier, Doane had asked Fanny to write a hymn for the home missions. He gave her a title—"Rescue the Perishing"—but for Fanny, the right words would not come. Leading the lad to Jesus gave her inspiration, and before going to bed, she wrote:

> Rescue the perishing,
> Care for the dying,
> Snatch them in pity from sin and the
>   grave;
> Weep o'er the erring one,
> Lift up the fallen,
> Tell them of Jesus, the mighty to save.

Thirty-five years later in Lynn, Massachusetts, Fanny spoke to an assembly of Christians at the YMCA. She told them of the incident with the lad and how it led to her writing "Rescue the Perishing." After the meeting, men passed to shake her hand, but one stopped and said, "Miss Crosby, I was that boy." Holding Fanny's hand with gentle affection, he added, "I have tried to live a steady Christian life ever since. If we never meet again, we will meet up yonder." Then he raised her hand to his lips and kissed it. Before she could recover from her surprise, the lad who had become a man of Christ was gone.

By the early 1870s, Fanny Crosby was well on the way to becoming the most famous hymnist in America. She continued to work with Dr.

Doane, who was now a lifelong friend, but composers of greater talent began calling at her apartment. They wanted Fanny's hymns—nobody else's. In 1875 Dwight L. Moody and Ira D. Sankey stepped into Fanny's life and brought her into the world of evangelism.

Moody, a lay preacher from Massachusetts who had become a YMCA evangelist in Chicago, had gone to Great Britain to conduct gospel campaigns in various cities. Thousands of people came to his meetings, many of them to profess faith in Christ. Everywhere Moody preached, Sankey performed as a marvelous baritone soloist. He sang many of Fanny's hymns, and soon "Pass Me Not, O Gentle Saviour" and "Safe in the Arms of Jesus" became popular in English homes. In 1870 Moody had found Sankey quite by accident during a YMCA convention in Indianapolis. Once Moody heard that wonderful baritone voice, he urged Sankey to give up his job in western Pennsylvania and help in the work of campaign evangelism. In 1875 they returned to New York as international figures and took the city by storm. By then, Sankey had begun to lose his voice, but during his years with Moody—which were many—he became an excellent organist.

Earlier that year Fanny turned fifty-five.

She and Van moved into rooms on the East Side
so they could be closer to Biglow and Main. She
spent several days a week at the office, but her
life was also changing. When evening came she
visited mission houses, slums, or prisons. Invitations came from afar, and she often traveled to
preach wherever God called her. Blindness never
stopped Fanny Crosby, nor did great distances.
She traveled alone and never let people treat
her like an invalid.

In 1875, when Moody and Sankey came
to Brooklyn, Fanny heard them preach and sing
for the first time. She did not meet them until
later, but she was familiar with Sankey's work.
Biglow and Main had recently published *Gospel
Hymns and Sacred Songs and Solos*, written by Sankey and Philip P. Bliss, and over time fifty million copies were sold. Fanny had hoped to work
with Bliss, but the composer died in a train accident. Bliss's death "cast a cloud" over Fanny's
spirit, but the Lord was working to bring her
together with Moody and Sankey.

Biglow and Main obtained a bundle of
Bliss's unfinished compositions and, with Fanny's
help, tried to select hymns for publication. When
Moody and Sankey came to New York in 1876,
Biglow invited them to the office. Much to their
surprise and delight, Moody and Sankey found

Fanny there. Sankey had sung her hymns and knew her work, and both times Moody had been in New York people had urged him to meet Fanny Crosby. They immediately began to work together, and the relationship would last their mutual lifetimes.

Sankey considered Fanny among the greatest living gospel songwriters—if not the greatest of them all. He encouraged her to write hundreds of new hymns, and when she did, he began to fill later issues of *Gospel Hymns and Sacred Songs and Solos* with more of her work. From Biglow and Main, Sankey obtained the rights to much of her earlier work and made it famous all over again.

With Fanny at his side, Sankey composed melodies to fit her gospel hymns. By then he had lost his voice and given up all attempts to sing. He had taught himself to play the organ— now he taught himself to write music. Fanny also began to compose music for her own poetry, so it became great fun to work together. Neither of them ever tried to produce complicated music, and often their melodies made wonderfully sweet gospel songs.

Some called Fanny the "queen of gospel song," but she did not limit herself to sacred songs. She wrote poetry for every occasion, and secular songs, and even a few love lyrics. When she preached, her message flowed like a hymn, and with age she became even more popular. Lines of people would stretch around the block to get inside and hear her. She spoke of joy in life, of God's great love, and of salvation through the blessings of Jesus Christ. When speaking, she always opened with "God bless your dear hearts! I'm so happy to be with you!" She could never see her audience, but she could feel them and knew their hearts. When speaking, she always carried a small Bible or booklet, and most of the time it was upside down. Some thought it contained her speech, written in Braille, but it was only a prop—something to hold in her hands. Fanny Crosby spoke from her heart.

Fanny became an inspiration to all she met, especially to the poor, the sick, and those in search of God's forgiveness. She would speak of her blindness as being "shut out of the world, and shut in with my Lord. I have served Him as I could."

She often spoke of the blessings of knowing her grandmother, who taught her the Bible, and how they sat together for hours in that wonderful old rocking chair. "The Lord is the sunshine of my soul," she would say. "I do not want to live for myself, but for Him." She would talk of her life—not of her sightlessness, but of God's great gifts. Knowing that most of her audience were people in some manner of need, she would say, "I always trusted that if it was God's will to give me what I wanted, He would do so, but if the Lord did not want me to have those things, it was best to not have them." Her message always struck home. Nobody in the audience could believe that Fanny would not want sight. But there she was, happy and filled with God's Spirit.

Somebody in the audience would usually ask that she recite some of her poems. Sometimes she would talk them through, and sometimes she would sing them. On many occasions, when she knew her audience, she made them up as she went. People would stand in the rain or shiver in the cold just to hear her speak. She preferred small audiences to large ones, but she took them all as they came. Without intending it, Fanny Crosby became one of the most effective evangelists of the day.

The Lord may have taken away Fanny's sight, but He gave her endless energy. She could outlast people twenty and thirty years younger. Sankey could never keep her busy enough, and Biglow and Main could never keep up with her output of hymns.

In 1877 Fanny began to set aside time for

short summer vacations. Instead of going on a tourist trip, she decided to attend the Methodist Episcopal Church camp at Ocean Grove, New Jersey. As usual, she traveled by herself. While there she lived in a small tent pitched on the beach. It could only be entered on one's hands and knees, but that was all right for fifty-seven-year-old Fanny. Several services, with much music and singing, were held each day. She had come as a guest of the camp and was often called upon to speak. Fanny got little rest, but she had a wonderful time. During the visit she met two composers—John R. Sweney and William J. Kirkpatrick—who pleaded with her to work with them.

Fanny knew Sweney by reputation, and at camp he led the songs. He taught music at the Pennsylvania Music Academy in Philadelphia and had formed his own band. He composed much of his own music and sometimes wrote hymns. During the summer he went from camp to camp and played light, happy melodies. Like Biglow and Main, he published hymnals and some of his songs contained Fanny's poetry.

Kirkpatrick worked with Sweney but was much better trained in compositions where voice, harmony, and the pipe organ were involved. In fact, "Kirkie," as Fanny called him, was a better musician than any composer for whom she had written. She enjoyed his company because he had a sense of humor that almost matched her own. Sweney was more businesslike, but she agreed to work with both of them. When Fanny returned to New York, she began filling her idle moments by supplying Sweney and "Kirkie" with new verses for their hymnals. During their long relationship, Fanny wrote more than a thousand poems for the hymnals edited by Sweney and Kirkpatrick.

She still had time to spare, and when Sankey announced that he intended to publish more gospel hymns, Fanny spent part of every week working with him. In the 1870s and 1880s—having become an evangelist—she produced much of her best work. With Fanny's help, Sankey eventually published six volumes of *Gospel Hymns and Sacred Songs and Solos*. But this was not the end of it.

Moody still traveled the country calling people to his flock of evangelists. Among them came George C. Stebbins, a self-taught musician and a marvelous choirmaster. He did not have Kirkpatrick's or Sankey's skills, but some of his music was pure delight. Moody connected him with Fanny, and though some of Stebbins's music lacked melody, she provided the polish whenever they were together. Two of Fanny's most famous pieces were written with Stebbins—"Saved by Grace," and "Jesus Is Calling."

> Jesus is tenderly calling thee home,
> Calling today, calling today,
> Why from the sunshine of love wilt thou
>   roam,
> Farther and farther away?
>
> Jesus is calling the weary to rest,
> Calling today, calling today,
> Bring Him thy burden and thou shalt be
>   blest;
> He will not turn thee away.

At the age of sixty, many people think of slowing down, but not Fanny. She had written so many hymns that it seemed—even to her—that nothing she wrote could any longer be new. So she looked for other work. She and Van moved to a dismal flat on Frankfort Street on the Lower East Side of New York. A few blocks away stretched the Bowery and some of Manhattan's worst slums.

Nobody but Fanny Crosby—sightless and growing old—would dare to live on such streets of rampant sin when they did not have to.

— 9 —

Leading Souls to Christ

*V*an, Fanny's husband, seemed willing to live wherever she took him. If he objected to being next to the New York slums, he never mentioned it. They lived among dance halls, taverns, alcoholics, ladies of the street, dancing bears, and small shops selling filthy pictures. On the Bowery, pickpockets and thugs made their living stealing from others, and castaways from the Civil War—men without arms, legs, or eyes— begged on the streets. Respectable people seldom passed through the area without a bodyguard. Yet Fanny chose to live there.

Long before the Lower East Side became a slum, Fanny had attended the John Street Methodist Church. For many years she had lived nearby when the neighborhood was poor, but not the filthy wreck it had now become. After she moved closer to Biglow and Main, she still returned to the Lower East Side to work with the missions and preach the Word. Now there were many missions, some funded by churches and others supported by donations from people like Fanny. She felt drawn to these streets of sins where she could serve people who had fallen from grace and hurry them back to the loving arms of Jesus.

Fanny became especially attached to Jerry McAuley, who founded the Water Street Mission. He had started life in a street gang, never received an education, served a five-year prison sentence for robbery, and drifted about as a bum until the John Street Methodist Church brought him to the Lord. Ten years later McAuley opened a larger mission, a three-story building on West 32nd Street where the homeless and unemployed could get food, clothing, shelter, and Christian guidance.

More missions sprang up in the area—Rev. Albert Rulifson's Bowery Mission, and Mrs. E. M. Whittemore's Door of Hope, a home providing for "fallen women." Fanny preached at all of them. Everyone knew she was blind, yet she often talked of "the joy it gives to walk in the light" and urged men to come forward and give their lives to Christ. Because drunks cluttered the Bowery, the missions were always trying to get them to sign a pledge to stop drinking. She often closed her service by saying, "If there is a man present who has gone just as far as he can go, he is the person with whom I want to shake hands."

One time an alcoholic sitting directly in front of the platform admitted that he was such a person, and Fanny asked if he would like to "come out and live a Christian life."

"Oh, what difference would it make?" he asked. "I have no friends—nobody cares for me."

"You are mistaken," Fanny replied, "for the Lord Jesus cares for you, and others care for you, too. Unless I had a deep interest in your soul's welfare I certainly would not be here talking with you on this subject."

Fanny recited some special lines of Scripture, and the man gave her words some thought. "If I come here to the meeting tomorrow and sign the pledge, will you come with me?" he asked.

"Yes, I will be here again," Fanny replied, "and though I do not discourage you from signing the pledge, it seems to me that the best pledge you can give is to yield yourself to God. Will you do it?"

The next evening he came again. Fanny took him by the hand and, like the great evangelists of the day, led him to the Lord. "That night," she said, "we saw the new light in his eyes and felt the change in his voice."

Fanny never called drinking alcoholic beverages a sin. She believed, however, that once individuals committed themselves to Jesus Christ, they would stop. Because of her soft approach to the problem, she had great success in helping to cure drunks. When Biglow and Main began publishing hymnals to fight alcoholism, Fanny filled them with temperance hymns.

Leading souls to Christ became the mission of her life. She did it with her hymns, her voice, her hands, and her blindness. She worked in the missions every night, first one and then another. Whenever a lost soul came forward and accepted Jesus, others followed. On Fanny's best nights dozens would be captured by her humble message.

Fanny deeply believed that "kindness in this world will do much to help others, not only to come into the light, but to grow in grace day by day. There are many timid souls whom we jostle morning and evening as we pass them by, but if only a kind word were spoken, they might be fully persuaded to accept the Lord."

She gave of her time freely and never took a penny for her mission work. Her reward came in many ways. She loved mankind, and those especially in need of God's great grace she loved even more. "Don't tell me a man is a sinner," she would say to others. "You can't save a man by telling him of his sins. He knows them already. Tell him there is pardon and love waiting for him. Win his confidence and make him understand that you believe in him, and never give him up."

Fanny practiced her own advice. She looked for troubled souls and often she found them in church—sometimes lurking in the shadows, sometimes seeking the light. One night she sensed that the man sitting in front of her had reached a crossroad in his life. As the service came to the close, she tapped him on the shoulder and whispered, "When the invitation is given, will you go to the altar?"

He hesitated, but then asked, "Will you go with me?"

"Yes," she replied. So they went together, and afterwards Fanny thanked the Lord for allowing her to bring to Him another "saved man."

All through the late 1870s and early 1880s Fanny became a familiar figure at the Bowery and the Water Street missions. She could not walk the street or sit in mission chapels without smelling alcohol, tobacco, and unwashed clothing that swarmed with vermin. She loved all those fallen souls, and during all the years she paced the streets, "Not one of them," she recalled, "was ever ugly to me."

When William Rock, president of the New York Surface Car Line, learned of Fanny's work with the missions, he invited her to his home. Many of his employees lived hard lives. They were a rough lot who worked seven days a week, swore at the passengers, and found little joy in life. When given a few hours leisure, many of them would head for the gin mills in the Bowery and get too drunk to come to work. Rock believed that a little spiritual guidance would set them straight, and he asked Fanny to provide it.

Fanny, of course, agreed. Rock paid his conductors and drivers to come to her Sunday service and provided a room for them at the car station. "Only a few came at first," Fanny recalled, "but finally the little room was filled with 'railroad' boys." Her services became so successful that the "boys" helped form the Railroad Branch of the YMCA. They set up a national office in Hoboken, New Jersey, and soon spread throughout the country. For the rest of her active life, Fanny became the YMCA's regular speaker on the East Coast. She never forgot her "railroad boys," and when she became too frail to travel, she wrote a tribute in their honor:

> How I would like to shake your hands,
>   And greet you one by one;

But we are now too far apart,
   And this cannot be done.
Yet I can hope, and wish, and pray
   That heaven's eternal joys
May fall like dew upon your heads,
   My noble railroad boys.

During the many years she spent among the missions, Fanny continued to work for Biglow and Main. Often they placed heavy demands upon her, sometimes asking for poems on subjects that gave her no inspiration. She always needed money, and she was growing older, but she never seemed to tire. Public appearances and social work took so much of her time during the day that she never started to write hymns until after midnight. She wrote what came to her mind, and Biglow and Main did not always get what they wanted on time.

Fanny loved her times of precious silence. She could open her heart to the Lord so deeply that she felt the presence of Christ and His angels in her heart. She could hear the "Celestial Choir" singing in the heavens and feel her soul move outwards until it merged with the beautiful sound. At times she felt the presence of her grandmother, and after her mother died at the age of ninety-one, they would all come together and unite in Fanny's midnight prayers.

Poems of great inspiration flowed from her devotions. Sometimes they appeared in a dreamy way, flowing out from a valley of silence where life's troubles took shelter:

> In the hush of the Valley of Silence,
> I dream all the songs that I sing,
> And the music floats down the dim valley
> Till each finds a word for a wing,
> That to men, like the dove of the Deluge,
> The message of peace they may bring.

One late night after prayer Fanny felt her mother's presence. Pieces of a poem collected in her mind and she fell asleep. When she awoke in the morning, the verse had come together and arranged itself in her memory. When she reached the office of Biglow and Main she dictated the lines to the clerk—a tribute to her mother:

> Her voyage in life is ended,
>   Her anchor firmly cast,
> Her bark that many a storm has braved
>   Is safe in port at last.
> Surrounded by her treasured ones,
>   Our mother passed away
> Beneath the golden sunset
>   Of summer's brightest day.

Oh, Mother, we are coming;
The time will not be long
Till we shall clasp thy hand again,
And join the blessed song.
The sheaf of wheat is garnered,
The sickle's work is done,
And everlasting glory
Through Christ her soul has won.

Biglow and Main, and most other publishers, paid Fanny a dollar or two (a day's wage) for each hymn. No matter how successful the hymn became, she never received another cent. The words became the property of the composer, who often earned little more than Fanny, and the publishing company pocketed all of the profit. As Fanny's hymns became more popular, her friends urged her to demand more money. "Safe in the Arms of Jesus" became so well known that it was translated into every language spoken in the Christian world. "Blessed Assurance," written for Sankey and published by Moody, is still sung, as is "Pass Me Not, O Gentle Saviour." But Fanny never wrote for wealth. "It is God's work," she would say. If she could lead lost souls to the Lord through her hymns, that would be payment enough.

For all of her life Fanny remained poor.

Whenever she had money, she gave it away—sometimes more than she could afford. Once she made the mistake of giving away her rent money. When the day came to pay the rent, she prayed for it. A man came to her door, thrust the exact amount—ten dollars—into her hand, said nothing, and left. That night Fanny offered prayers of thanks during her midnight devotions. And then, before she fell asleep, wrote the hymn "All the Way My Saviour Leads Me."

Fanny lived life as her Saviour led her. She wrote hymns to bring people to salvation through Jesus Christ. She worked in the missions, seeing the conversion of many lost souls who wasted their lives in the slums. Sankey once told Fanny, "You have been the means of cheering tens of thousands trudging along the highways of life." Later, after he returned from a visit abroad, he told her that "Safe in the Arms of Jesus" had reached out to thousands in Great Britain and brought them back to the church.

In the slums of New York, the singing of her hymns in mission houses brought thousands more off the streets and into new lives of hope. Fanny never forgot one poor, hungry youngster who stumbled inside during a service. When the hymn ended, he went to Fanny and said, "I was just ready to perish, but that hymn, by the grace of God, saved me." Fanny hugged the lad and asked him to tell his story to the people seated at the mission. By the time he finished, tears fell in all corners of the room. Scenes like this occurred every night—lost souls searching for love and hope in Christ.

Fanny not only pointed souls to Jesus, she often saw them converted into mission workers. Every person who accepted work with the missions brought more to the faith. One saved soul could reach out to hundreds of others, so for Fanny, every person in need of salvation became another potential worker for God.

In 1884 Jerry McAuley, still a young man, died from tuberculosis. Sam Hadley took over the Water Street Mission, and it was there that Fanny met Sam's brother, Henry Harrison Hadley. Henry had been a distinguished colonel in the Civil War and a lawyer in peacetime. Drunkenness cost him his law practice, so he started a newspaper in New York. Fanny sent him dozens of poems preaching against alcoholism. The colonel printed them in his paper, but they did him little good. At his brother's Water Street Mission, Henry listened to Fanny's many sermons on the evils of drinking—and she finally got him to pray in earnest for delivery from alcohol. The cure worked. He woke one morning and never touched another drop. Over the next sixteen years, Henry established sixty rescue missions and became a Christian leader. Fanny helped save Henry from the curse of drink, and Henry became a servant of Jesus.

Later, in the 1890s, one of Fanny's remarkable friends was Gerhard J. Schilling, a German who had been cast out of Burma for his Christian beliefs. After reaching New York, he entered divinity school and soon met Fanny at one of the missions. Though Schilling was forty years younger than Fanny, they became great friends. He picked her up in his carriage every Sunday and Wednesday and together they went to church. He loved her grace almost as much as he loved her hymns. In 1894 Schilling decided to go back to Burma as a missionary. To explain his sudden decision, he said, "The inspiration to return to Burma came from Fanny Crosby." This time he stayed, translating the Bible and Christian hymns into Burma's native language.

Because she could not see, physical contact was very important to Fanny. She hugged the drunks and Bowery bums as readily as she did her sisters, Carrie and Julie, or her many hundreds of friends. Her hymns were filled with physical touching and feeling, like "Safe in the Arms of Jesus" and "Pass Me Not." In "I Am

Thine, O Lord," she wrote: "But I long to rise in the arms of faith / And be closer drawn to thee. / Draw me nearer, nearer, blessed Lord." Even in her early poems, the sensation of touch and feel was strong. In "Grandma's Rocking Chair," she wrote, "In her loving arms she held me, / And beneath her patient care, / I was borne away to dreamland, / In her dear old rocking chair."

Fanny worked in the missions for as many years as she could. After reaching the age of sixty-three, the harsh streets of the slums were beginning to wear her down. She and Van finally moved uptown to First Avenue and 79th Street, but her work was not done. Age had begun to take its toll on her body, but her mind and her spirit were still active. There were other mountains to climb and souls to be saved, especially in Manhattan.

—10—

Thirty More Years

On March 24, 1884, Biglow and Main hosted the first annual Fanny Crosby Birthday Party as a tribute to her twenty years of work. During that time, she had written for them more than 3,000 hymns. Many of her friends and their wives attended, among them Ira Sankey, who was gradually losing his eyesight. Those who missed the party sent poems, some humorous but all expressing their love and affection for the grand old lady of gospel hymns. Little did they know that she would outlive most of them.

During the 1880s Fanny continued to supply hymns for Biglow and Main, Sankey, Kirkpatrick, Sweney, and others. These included many favorites like "Tell Me the Story of Jesus," which was influenced by Matthew 18:3, Acts 8:35, and Philippians 3:8. Many of her hymns were based on passages of Scripture. She especially liked Psalms, which she used in "Redeemed" (Psalm 107:2). In "He Hideth My Soul" she may have taken the theme from Psalm 27:5 and Psalm 94:22, and "To God Be the Glory" came from Psalm 126:3. Scripture gave her inspiration, but she seldom just copied the words. Instead, she concentrated on the message and, with music, made it joyful and easy to understand.

As the 1890s approached, Fanny wrote fewer hymns. There seemed to be nothing to say that she had not already said! To occupy some of her time, she returned to writing secular lyrics. She worked with Howard Doane on the Christmas cantata *Santa Claus*, and with Hart P. Danks on *Zanie*. Some of her friends thought she should stick with hymns, but Fanny believed there were other ways to express the work of good over evil. If some people could not be reached through hymns, then Fanny would try to reach them through popular music.

Though she continued to write hymns, few ever became as popular as those she wrote from the 1860s to the 1880s. By the 1890s she had composed so many hymns that she could not remember them all. Sometimes when she heard them sung, she could not even recognize her own work. When pressed to write "just one more hymn," she would always pray and wait for inspiration. Sometimes it came when she least expected it. Even as she worked through her seventies, the Lord would not let her talent go to waste. Sweney wanted something tender, so she wrote "My Saviour First of All." Soon the hymn captured the hearts of English-speaking people around the world. During the same period she wrote "Some Day" for Biglow and Main as a tribute to her cousin, Dr. Howard Crosby, who had recently died. Biglow paid her the usual two dollars and put the words in his vault with thousands of others. A few years later it would be found and published. In the meantime she tucked the poem in her memory, never expecting to use it as a hymn.

"Some Day" held a special place in Fanny's heart. She had lost her mother, her cousin, both of her brothers-in-law, and many close, loving friends—and "some day" she would join them all. At the time Fanny sold the lyrics to Biglow and Main, Van was not well. She could not care for him, so he moved in with a family named Underhill to live out the remainder of his life in a more comfortable apartment. Fanny called on him often, but their relationship had long ago become one of devoted friendship. Van had always been frail, and their life together had never been quite the same after their baby died. But true to her promise to Van's mother, she always looked after him and was grateful to the Underhills for giving him a better home.

With Van gone, Ira Sankey worried about Fanny living alone in a city so rapidly changing. He spent much of his time with her, and during the summers he would take her to the Northfield Bible Conference in Massachusetts as his guest. She loved being there but shied away from speaking. One day during a service on the Holy Spirit, Sankey touched her arm and said, "Will you say something? There is a request from the audience that you speak."

Fanny replied, "Please, Sankey, I cannot speak before such an array of talent."

The pastor leading the service then came to her and asked, "Fanny, do you speak to please man or to please God?"

The question startled her. "Why, I hope . . . to please God."

"Well, then," said the minister, "go out and do your duty."

While being led to the platform Fanny had little time to arrange her thoughts, so she said a few words in praise of God and then recited "Some Day," her heart's song.

Some day the silver cord will break,
And I no more as now shall sing;
But, oh, the joy when I shall wake
Within the palace of the King!

Some day my earthly house will fall;
  I cannot tell how soon 'twill be;
But this I know—my All in All
  Has now a place in heaven for me.

By the time Fanny finished all four stanzas she had the gathering in tears. Sankey, who was working on a new hymnal with Biglow and Main, located the poem in the publisher's files, where for three years it had been placed with hundreds of others. Sankey sent the poem to Stebbins, who asked Fanny for a two-line chorus, so she added the following words:

And I shall see Him face to face,
And tell the story—Saved by grace.

Stebbins composed the music, giving it a slow and almost mournful melody. He then returned the completed hymn to Biglow and Main for publication. When the hymn reached the churches in 1894, it grew in popularity with its new title, "Saved by Grace." On the streets and in the theaters it became one of the hit songs of the Gay Nineties. At the age of seventy-four, Fanny Crosby had written one of her last popular hymns.

One bright spot in Fanny's life was the

return of Grover Cleveland to New York. He had finished his term as president, moved to Madison Avenue, and invited Fanny to his home. They had a marvelous time recalling their days together at the New York Institute for the Blind. Fanny remembered Cleveland as a tall, skinny prankster. He had grown into a large, robust man with thin hair. She enjoyed his wonderful sense of humor, and over the years of their renewed friendship they shared many happy moments together.

Despite her popularity, Fanny remained poor. After her mother died she let the entire estate go to Carrie and Julie. On the streets of New York everybody recognized her—a tiny, stooped lady fitted with old dresses and tattered bonnets saved from the 1840s. She still preached at the many mission houses operating near the Bowery and probably acquired some of her clothes from public donations. She also still worked for Biglow and Main, though not very hard, and for Sweney and Kirkpatrick. They all paid her two dollars for every hymn, even though most of them went into a file and never surfaced again. For a blind person approaching the age of eighty, she was still more active than most people twenty years younger and continued to conduct services and give speeches at the Railroad Branch of the YMCA.

Fanny served the Lord for most of her long life but in the 1890s reached an age when she had to slow down. She never worried about her own welfare, always believing that God would provide. When in prayer, she put her needs aside for those in greater need. Van, who was eleven years younger than Fanny, had always helped with the expenses, but he was with the Underhills and could no longer work. Fanny would neither ask anyone for help nor take money—though she needed it—so the Lord stepped in and called her friends to the rescue. Ira Sankey, Howard Doane, John Sweney, Robert Lowry, and Biglow and Main had all become wealthy musicians or publishers because of Fanny's hymns. Few of them were any longer in good health. One by one, they began asking themselves why Fanny should not be as comfortable and as well off as they were. Each began working in his own way to help her, but not in a way to make his generosity appear as charity. Sankey had been looking after her for years, but now the time had come for everyone to help.

Mr. Moody came back to New York to create another "great awakening," but the people of the Gay Nineties were not interested in Christian revival. By 1896 he admitted that his campaign had been an enormous failure. The missions were still filled with the homeless and the wrecks of society, but support had fallen off and some of the missions were forced to close. Moody became furious with the city's churches, but it did no good. To console himself, he would sit at the organ for hours and sing Fanny's "Saved by Grace" until tears ran down his cheeks.

Moody's life as an evangelist had neared its end, but his great love for Fanny brought him once more to the office of Biglow and Main. Instead of their paying her two dollars for each hymn, he suggested that Biglow and Main pay her a salary of eight dollars a week. She had never made much more than four hundred dollars a year, so this, Moody argued, would give her a permanent income. At the time, Fanny was approaching eighty and appeared to be in very poor health. Once during this period she suffered a heart attack and lapsed into a partial coma. Because Van could no longer give her support, Biglow and Main agreed with Moody and put her on a permanent salary of eight dollars a week for as long as she lived. Fanny soon recovered and lived another eighteen years!

During this time Dr. Lowry—now old and deaf—also became concerned about Fanny's welfare. He knew that she had hundreds of poems in Biglow and Main's vault. He also knew of the three books of poetry she had written many years ago. New hymnals were not selling well, so Lowry convinced Biglow and Main to search their files for Fanny's poems. By adding a few selections from her three earlier books, Biglow and Main combined the best of Fanny's poetry into a new book titled *Bells at Evening*. It contained 224 pages and sold for fifty cents a copy. Over the years, Biglow and Main sold several editions and gave all the profits to Fanny.

Others came to her rescue. Phoebe Knapp, one of Fanny's oldest and wealthiest friends, had often tried to give her money but never succeeded. Phoebe thought the world should know the story of Fanny Crosby. She went to Will Carleton, author of several books and editor of the magazine *Every Where*, and urged him to see Fanny and write the story of her early life. Carleton had always admired Fanny, so he agreed to see her about doing her story in serial form. When he visited her one-room apartment in a poor Brooklyn neighborhood, he could not believe the shabby conditions in which the famous hymnist lived. He immediately agreed to pay her ten dollars for each article, and *Every Where* ran the serial for many months. In 1903 Carleton brought out *Fanny Crosby's Life-Story* in book form and kept it in print for as long as he could.

When writing Fanny's story, Carleton came to the conclusion that Biglow and Main had never paid her enough. Because of Carleton's claim, Phoebe Knapp came to the same conclusion and spoke out against Fanny's lifelong employers. This offended Doane, who composed much of her music, and Biglow and Main, who published it. Few of Fanny's friends ever understood that she lived poor by her own choice. No matter how much money she earned, Fanny would always give away whatever she did not need. By the time she reached the age of eighty, Fanny had plenty of money coming in. She may have kept a little more in her cookie jar, but most of the surplus went to the missions.

In 1898 Fanny came down with pneumonia and her health collapsed for the third time in her life. Her sisters, Julie and Carrie, rushed to Brooklyn and brought her home to Bridgeport. Julie looked after Fanny for the rest of her life. Ira Sankey paid the rent for a pleasant five-room apartment, but they kept the secret from Fanny. Carrie became Fanny's secretary but could never run her life.

As soon as Fanny recovered, she went back to work writing hymns and traveling the country. When she spoke at conferences, people were always struck by her strong voice and composed spirit. Though obviously stooped and quite old, there was always something youthful about the "queen of gospel music." Her presence and carriage, the musical voice, and the marvelous message made her one of the most sought-after speakers for every occasion. She believed that as long as she kept busy, she would always stay young. If she abandoned her work, she would not live a year. Her vigor astounded her friends, and her sorrow was to come in losing them.

John Sweney suffered a stroke and died in April of 1899. Lowry died in November, Moody a month later. Then Sankey, whose eyes had been failing, went stone-blind. Van died in the summer of 1902, at the Underhills', after a prolonged bout with cancer. Though they had not been together for many years, Fanny still loved and missed him. The turn of the century had indeed been filled with sorrow.

When Ira Sankey lost his sight, he tried to keep the fact from the public, but it only made matters worse. He settled into a life of deep depression and no longer attempted to work. Fanny visited often, cheering his spirits. He could still play the organ, so they would sit together to harmonize and to remember the happier days. But as soon as Fanny departed, he would return to his chair and wait to die.

Yet Fanny lived on. New composers came

on the scene, men like Charles H. Gabriel who wrote simple music with a lilt, and Ira Allan Sankey, the son of her lifelong friend. Fanny wrote hymns for both men. She also wrote for several other musicians, some of whom she met as organists playing in the mission houses. When Allan Sankey went to work for Biglow and Main, Fanny once again increased her output of hymns. She was now well into her eighties, and her hymns reflected how she looked upon life. With Allan Sankey she wrote her last popular hymn—"Never Give Up."

> Never be sad or desponding
> If thou hast faith to believe;
> Grace, for the duties before thee,
> Ask of thy God and receive.

Chorus:
> Never give up, never give up,
> Never give up to thy sorrows,
> Jesus will bid them depart;
> Trust in the Lord, trust in the Lord,
> Sing when your trials are greatest,
> Trust in the Lord and take heart!

Fanny never gave up. Blinded since infancy, the only light she ever saw as an adult was the light of God. It served her well. On March 24, 1905, she turned eighty-five, and the churches in New York proclaimed it Fanny Crosby Day. On Sunday, March 26, millions filled churches all over America to sing her hymns. Music poured through the doors and onto the streets, and lifted up the spirits of those who could find no space inside. A collection in her honor was taken up in every church, and offerings of love totaling thousands of dollars were sent to her in New York. This time she had to accept, but the money would not stay with her long. She kept a little for her sisters and gave the rest away.

In 1905 she began writing her autobiography—*Memories of Eighty Years*. In 1906 the book went into print, but with happiness came tragedy. Carrie died of cancer, and months later the Lord took Ida, Julie's daughter. Fanny kept telling herself, "Never give up, never give up," and though eighty-six years old, she pulled herself together and continued to produce about fifty hymns a year.

Fanny spent the rest of her life with friends, Henry and Florence Booth, who lived on Wells Street in Bridgeport. She still traveled and worked at the missions and continued to do so until 1914, when she suffered another heart attack. When the doctors told her she could not live much longer, she welcomed the news with joy. Her old friend, Howard Doane, was dying, too. They had worked together for more than sixty years. They might never make music on earth again, but Fanny believed that the Lord would call upon their talents in a better place.

In making arrangements for her death, Fanny made Julie promise not to buy an expensive headstone but to give the money saved to the Christian Union in Bridgeport. If her friends wanted to raise money in her memory, Fanny told Julie to let them set up a fund to build an infirmary for the Christian Union or found a home for elderly people. She then asked for a lawyer and made her will, leaving half of her estate to Julia and the other half to Florence Booth, who had cared for her for more than twelve years.

On the morning of February 12, 1915, at the age of ninety-four, Fanny Crosby suffered a massive cerebral hemorrhage and died an hour later. She went peacefully, and in God's great grace. Her work on earth had ended, but not her popularity. Her funeral was the largest Bridgeport had ever seen. Old friends and admirers flocked into the city to pay their last respects. Reverend H. A. Davenport of the People's Presbyterian Church gave the prayer, and the sanc-

tuary was filled with all of Fanny's favorite flowers—flowers such as she had first held as a blind
child and kept in her heart all of her life. The
choir sang "Safe in the Arms of Jesus," "Saved
by Grace," and many others of her hymns as
hundreds of people who loved her wept and remembered.

In one of the many eulogies spoken in tribute to Fanny Crosby, Dr. Brown faced the congregation and said, "You have come to pay tribute and to crown a friend. There must have been
a royal welcome when this queen of sacred song
burst the bonds of death and passed into the
glories of heaven."

As the people left the church, each received a violet. When passing the casket, they
laid the petals gently beside her, and Fanny Crosby
departed forever, asleep on a bed of flowers.

Afterword

*D*uring her lifetime, Fanny Crosby wrote more poems and hymns than anybody has been able to count. In her forty-seven years at Biglow and Main she wrote 6,000 hymns, though only about 2,000 were published. This was because she often wrote several poems for the same title, but the music composer would choose only one.

For Ira Sankey, George Stebbins, and John Sweney she wrote at least 4,000 more. Because she also composed for others, it is likely that she wrote as many as 12,000 hymns during her lifetime. The count becomes even more difficult because she wrote secular songs, operettas, and popular lyrics and used more than one hundred pen names.

When quite young she began writing poetry, never intending that her poems be set to music. She published her first book of poetry at the age of twenty-four while teaching at the New York Institute for the Blind—*The Blind Girl and Other Poems*—in 1844. This little book contained her best early poems—not all her poems. At the age of thirty-one she published *Monterey and Others Poems* (1851), and eight years later *A Wreath of Columbia's Flowers*. After writing the latter, she concentrated on hymns—but hymns were just another form of poetry. Some of her best work appeared in her last book of poetry, *Bells at Evening*, published in 1897. Fanny wrote thousands of poems which were never recorded and may never be found.

Fanny also composed music to some of her hymns. While she fingered out the melody on the piano, a clerk sat by her side and recorded the notes. To say that Fanny "wrote" something is not entirely accurate because she rarely picked up a pen and wrote anything. She put the verse together in her mind and dictated it. Clerks marveled at her ability to recite verse after verse without ever hesitating or making a change.

Fanny Crosby's one goal in life was to bring a million souls to God. In today's world, evangelists fill football stadiums for Christ, and pastors of all denominations use television to bring the message of salvation to those who cannot or will not attend church. Little Fanny Crosby—blind and poor—had none of those facilities or technical advantages. Instead, she captured her million souls through hymns and mission work—a few at a time—and spent most of her ninety-four years on earth doing it.

Today, her work still goes on. Hymnals in churches around the world still carry her spiritual messages in song. Her hymns are played on everything from grand old pipe organs to tiny spinet pianos. They are sung in great churches with choirs of hundreds and in small country chapels visited on Sundays by rural families with their children.

Though blind for life, Fanny Crosby used her years on earth to help millions of lost souls find Christ. Her last hymn, "Never Give Up," is a message of mission to all of us.

Safe in the Arms of Jesus

Fanny J. Crosby

William H. Doane

1. Safe in the arms of Je - sus, Safe on His gen - tle breast, There by His
2. Safe in the arms of Je - sus, Safe from cor - rod - ing care, Safe from the
3. Je - sus, my heart's dear ref - uge, Je - sus has died for me; Firm on the

love o'er - shad - ed, Sweet-ly my soul shall rest. Hark! 'tis the voice of
world's temp - ta - tions, Sin can - not harm me there. Free from the blight of
Rock of A - ges, Ev - er my trust shall be. Here let me wait with

an - gels, Borne in a song to me, O - ver the fields of glo - ry,
sor - row, Free from my doubts and fears; On - ly a few more tri - als,
pa - tience, Wait till the night is o'er; Wait till I see the morn - ing

Chorus

O - ver the jas - per sea.
On - ly a few more tears! Safe in the arms of Je - sus, Safe on His
Break on the gold - en shore.

gen - tle breast, There by His love o'er-shad - ed, Sweet-ly my soul shall rest.